Klas Pontus Arnoldson

Pax mundi

a concise account of the progress of the movement for peace by means of

arbitration, neutralization, international law and disarmament

Klas Pontus Arnoldson

Pax mundi
*a concise account of the progress of the movement for peace by means of arbitration,
neutralization, international law and disarmament*

ISBN/EAN: 9783337367527

Printed in Europe, USA, Canada, Australia, Japan

Cover: Foto ©Suzi / pixelio.de

More available books at **www.hansebooks.com**

PAX MUNDI

A CONCISE ACCOUNT OF THE PROGRESS OF THE MOVEMENT FOR PEACE
BY MEANS OF ARBITRATION, NEUTRALIZATION, INTERNATIONAL LAW AND DISARMAMENT

BY

K. P. ARNOLDSON
Member of the Second Chamber of the Swedish Riksdag

AUTHORIZED ENGLISH EDITION

WITH AN INTRODUCTION BY THE BISHOP OF DURHAM

London

SWAN SONNENSCHEIN & CO.
PATERNOSTER SQUARE
1892

CONTENTS.

PREFATORY NOTE.

THIS little work, written by one who has long
been known as a consistent and able advocate
of the views herein maintained, has been translated by a lady who has already rendered great
services to the cause, in the belief that it will
be found useful by the increasing number of
those who are interested in the movement for
the substitution of Law for War in international
affairs.

J. F. G.

INTRODUCTION TO THE ENGLISH EDITION.

It is natural that the advocates of international Peace should sometimes grow discouraged and impatient through what they are tempted to consider the slow progress of their cause. Sudden outbursts of popular feeling, selfish plans for national aggrandisement, unremoved causes of antipathy between neighbours, lead them to overlook the general tendency of circumstances and opinions which, when it is regarded on a large scale, is sufficient to justify their loftiest hopes. It is this general tendency of thought and fact, corresponding to the maturer growth of peoples, which brings to us the certain assurance that the Angelic Hymn which welcomed the Birth of Christ advances, slowly it may be as men count slowness, but at least unmistakably, towards fulfilment. There are pauses and interruptions in the movement; but, on the whole, no one who patiently regards the course of human history can doubt that we are drawing nearer from generation to generation to a practical sense of that brotherhood and

that solidarity of men—both words are necessary — which find their foundation and their
crown in the message of the Gospel.

Under this aspect the Essay of Mr. Arnoldson is of great value, as giving a calm and
comprehensive view of the progress of the
course of Peace during the last century, and of
the influences which are likely to accelerate its
progress in the near future.

Mr. Arnoldson, who, as a member of the
Swedish Parliament, is a practical statesman,
indulges in no illusions. The fulness with
which he dwells on the political problems of
Scandinavia shows that he is not inclined to
forget practical questions under the attraction
of splendid theories. He marks the chief
dangers which threaten the peace of Europe,
without the least sign of dissembling their
gravity. And looking steadily upon them, he
remains bold in hope; for confidence in a great
cause does not come from disregarding or dis-
paraging the difficulties by which it is beset,
but from the reasonable conviction that there
are forces at work which are adequate to overcome them.

We believe that it is so in the case of a

policy of Peace; and the facts to which Mr. Arnoldson directs attention amply justify the belief. It is of great significance that since 1794 there have been "at least sixty-seven instances in which disputes of a menacing character have been averted by arbitration"; and perhaps the unquestioning acceptance by England of the Genevan award will hereafter be reckoned as one of her noblest services to the world. It is no less important that since the principle of arbitration was solemnly recognised by the Congress of Paris in 1856, arbitral clauses have been introduced into many treaties, while the question of establishing a universal system of international arbitration has been entertained and discussed sympathetically by many parliaments.

At the same time Mr. Arnoldson justly insists on the steady increase of the power of neutrals. Without accepting the possibility of "a Neutral League," he points out how a necessary regard to the interests of neutrals restrains the powers which are meditating war. And I cannot but believe that he is right when he suggests that the problems of the neutralization of Scandinavia, of Alsace and

Lorraine, of the Balkan States, of the Bosphorus and Dardanelles, demand the attention of all who seek to hasten " the coming peace."

It would be easy to overrate the direct value of these facts; but their value as signs of the direction in which public opinion is rapidly moving can. hardly be overrated. They are symptoms of a growing recognition of the obligations of man to man, and of people to people, of our common human interests and of our universal interdependence.

I should not lay great stress on the deterrent power of the prospect of the ruinous losses and desolations likely to follow from future wars. A great principle might well demand from a nation great sacrifices; and the very strength of a policy of Peace lies in the postponement of material interests to human duties. But none the less the wide expansion of commercial and social intercourse, joint enterprises, even rivalries not always ungenerous, exercise a salutary influence upon the feeling of nation for nation, and make what were once regarded as natural animosities no longer possible.

Under the action of these forces we are learning more and more to endeavour to regard

debated questions from the point of sight of
our adversaries, to take account of their reasonable aspirations, to make allowance for their
difficulties, even to consider how they can best
render their appropriate service to the race,
while we strive no less resolutely to keep or to
secure the power of fulfilling our own. We
could not regard our enemies as our grand-
fathers regarded theirs. Already the conviction
begins to make itself felt that the loss of one
people is the loss of all.

Meanwhile the growth of popular power and
popular responsibility brings a wider and more
collective judgment to bear upon national
questions. The masses of peoples have more
in common than their leaders, among whom
individual character has fuller development.
The average opinion of men, when the facts
are set forth, responds to pleas of fellowship
and righteousness, and tends to become domi-
nant.

Such influences in favour of international
Peace spring out of steady movements which,
as they continue, will increase them. The past
does not limit their power, but simply reveals
the line of their action. Above all, they cor-

respond with that view of our Christian faith which the Holy Spirit is disclosing to us by means of the trials of our age. Through many sorrows and many disappointments we are learning that the fact of the Incarnation assures to us the unity of men and classes and nations; and a wider study of history, which is now possible, shows that the course of events makes for the establishment of that unity for which we were created.

I cannot therefore but hope that the Essay of Mr. Arnoldson, which gives substantial evidence of the reality and growth of this movement towards Peace, will confirm in courage ous and patient labour for an assured end all who join in the prayer that it may please God "to give to all nations unity, peace, and concord."

B. F. DUNELM.

AUCKLAND CASTLE,
October 14*th*, 1891.

PAX MUNDI.

INTRODUCTION.

It was the small beginning of a great matter when, on December 22nd, 1620, a hundred Puritans landed from the ship *Mayflower* upon the rocky shore of the New World, having, during the voyage, signed a constitution to be observed by the colonists.

These pious pilgrims were guided by the conception of religious freedom which should construct for them there a new kingdom. They had, say the annalists of the colony, crossed the world's sea and had reached their goal; but no friend came forth to meet them; no house offered them shelter. And it was midwinter. Those who know that distant clime, know how bitter are the winters and how dangerous the storms which at that season ravage the coast. It were bad enough in similar circumstances to travel in a well-known region; but how much worse when it is a question of seeking to settle on an entirely unknown shore.

They saw around them only a bare, cheerless country, filled with wild animals and inhabited by men of questionable disposition and in unknown numbers. The country was frozen and overgrown with woods and thickets. The whole aspect was wild; and behind them lay the measureless ocean, which severed them from the civilized world. Comfort and hope were to be found only in turning their gaze heavenward.

That they did conquer that ungrateful land. and open the way for the boundless stream of immigration which for wellnigh three centuries has unceasingly poured in, must find its explanation in the faith that upheld their ways amid the dangers of the wilderness, amid the hunger, cold, and all manner of disheartening things, and gave them that power which removed mountains and made the desert bloom.

These Puritans, strong in faith, were the founders of the New World's greatness; and their spirit spoke out to the Old World in the greeting with which the President of the United States consecrated the first transatlantic telegraph cable in 1866 :—

"Glory be to God in the highest, and on earth peace, goodwill to men."

When this message came to us, the roar of cannon was but newly hushed, and the man of "blood and iron" had victoriously set his foot upon one of Europe's great powers; the same Austria which since then has, by the Triple Alliance, united its warlike strength with Germany.

But that message has not been an unheeded sound to all; especially to those whose warning voices the people never listen to before the misfortune falls, but who are always justified after it has struck. Yes! perchance in the near future it may again appeal to their reason, and find a hearing only when Europe has fallen into untold miseries after another war.

While menacing forebodings of this long expected war were spreading in the summer of 1887 through various parts of our continent, a little company of courageous men, strong in faith, like the pious pilgrims of the *Mayflower*, gathered together for the voyage across the

sea to the New World, there to lay the foundation of a lasting work for peace.

Their first object was to present to the
President of the United States and to Congress an address aiming at the establishment
of a Court of Arbitration, qualified to deal with
disputes which might arise between Great
Britain and the United States of North America.
In that address, signed by 270 Members of
the British Parliament, allusion was made to
the resolutions on peace which from time to
time had been brought into Congress ; and
those who undersigned it declared themselves
ready to bring all their influence to bear in
inducing the Government of Great Britain to
accept the proposition which should come from
the Congress.   Amongst those who signed it
were, besides many distinguished Members of
the House of Commons, several peers, including some of the bishops.

The address was presented to President
Cleveland on October 31st, by a deputation of
twelve Members of Parliament, whose spokesman, Mr. Andrew Carnegie, in his introductory
speech, said : " Few events in the world's
history would rank with the making of such

a treaty. Perhaps only two in our own
country's history could fitly be compared with
it. Washington's administration established the
republic; Lincoln's administration abolished
human slavery. We fondly hope, sir, that it
may be reserved for yours to conclude a treaty
not only with the government of the other
great English-speaking nation, but with other
lands as well, which shall henceforth and for
ever secure to those nations the blessings of
mutual peace and goodwill. The conclusion of
such a treaty will have done much to remove
from humanity its greatest stain—the killing of
man by man. And we venture to hope, that if
the two great nations here represented set such
an example, other nations may be induced to
follow it, and war be thus ultimately banished
from the face of the earth."

In the President's favourable answer he mentioned that no nation in its moral and material
development could show more victories in the
domain of peace than the American; and it
appeared to him that the land which had
produced such proofs of the blessings of peace,
and therefore need not fear being accused of
weakness, must be in a specially favourable

position to listen to a proposal like the present ; wherefore he received it with pleasure and satisfaction.

A week later, Nov. 8th, the son-in-law of Queen Victoria, the Marquis of Lorne, presided over a great meeting in London, at which many eminent men were present. The chairman emphatically remarked in his speech, that the settlement of international disputes by a Court of Arbitration has the advantage that, through the delay which is necessary, the first excitement has time to cool. The meeting declared itself unanimously in favour of the proposed memorial. Thereupon followed many similar expressions of opinion in England, whilst simultaneously in twenty of the largest cities of North America mass meetings were held, which with unanimous enthusiasm gave adhesion to the cause, and petitions of the same character flowed in to the President and Congress from the various parts of the great republic.

Encouraged by these preparatory movements amongst the two great English-speaking peoples, M. Frederic Passy, with other Members of the Legislative Assembly of France, placed himself at the head of a movement to petition the French Government, requesting that it should conclude an Arbitration Treaty with the United States.

Such a memorial, bearing the signatures of 112 deputies and 16 senators, was received with much interest by the President.

On April 21st, 1888, Passy and forty-four other deputies moved a resolution in the Chamber to the same effect; and the idea has been carried forward in many ways since then, especially by a petition to the President of the United States from three International Congresses held in Paris, June 23rd–30th, 1889.

ARBITRATION.

Should these efforts lead in the near future to the intended result, International Law would thereby have made an important progress.

It can no longer be denied that International Law does actually exist; but we undervalue its significance because we are impatient. We do not notice the advances it has made because they have been small; but they have been numerous; and slowly, step by step, international jurisprudence has progressed. This affects not only the awakening sense of justice and acknowledged principles, but also their application, which from the days of Hugo Grotius, 250 years ago, down to Martens, Bluntschli, Calvo, and other most distinguished jurists of our day, has been the subject of great scholarly activity, by means of which the various regulations of jurisprudence have little by little been pieced together into a foundation and substance of universally accepted law.

What has been most generally done to gain the object in view has been the INSERTION OF ARBITRAL CLAUSES in treaties which were being concluded or had already been concluded in reference to other questions.   In this direction SIGNOR MANCINI of Italy has been especially active.   As during the time he was Minister of Foreign Affairs he had the concluding of a great number of treaties between Italy and other countries, he made use of the opportunity to insert into almost all—in nineteen instances[1]—an arbitral clause.

We have examples of treaties with such clauses in the commercial treaty between Italy and England, 1883 ; Norway, Sweden, and Spain, by a supplement in 1887 ; also England and Greece, 1886.   According to the first two agreements, all disputes about the right understanding of the treaties shall be settled by arbitration, as soon as it becomes apparent that it is vain to hope for a friendly arrangement.   In the Greco-English treaty it is further stipulated that all disputes which directly or indirectly may arise in consequence of that

---

[1] Mazzoleni, in his " L'Italia nel movimento per la Pace," gives twenty instances.   See pp. 58, 59.   TRANS.

treaty always shall, if they cannot be amicably
arranged, be referred to a committee of arbitration, which shall be nominated by each party
with a like number of members ; also that if
this committee cannot agree, there shall be
appointed a tribunal of arbitration, whose decision both nations bind themselves to accept.

The idea of concluding distinct TREATIES OF
ARBITRATION, or of giving a widely extended
range to arbitral clauses, so that they should
affect the whole relation of the contracting
parties to one another, is comparatively new.

So far as I know, Mr. William Jay was the
first who in modern times advocated this idea,
in a work which came out in New York in
1842, and in which he proposed : that in the
next treaty between, for example, the United
States and France, it should be stated that in
case any dispute should arise between the two
nations, not only in respect of the interpretation
of that treaty, but also in respect of any other
subject whatever, the dispute should be settled
by means of an arbitration by one or more
friendly powers.

A similar proposition was presented to Lord
Clarendon in 1853. By sending a deputation

to the plenipotentiaries at the CONGRESS AT
PARIS in 1856, the English "Peace Society":
succeeded in inducing them to introduce into
one of the protocols a solemn recognition of
the principle of Arbitration. In the name of
their governments they expressed the wish that
the states between which any serious misunderstanding should arise, should, as far as circumstances permitted, submit the question to the
arbitration of a friendly power before resorting
to arms. This proposition, which was unanimously adopted, was made by Lord Clarendon,
the representative of England, and supported
by the emissaries of France, Prussia, and Italy,
—Walewsky, Manteufel, and Cavour.

But the first movement in favour of independent Treaties of Arbitration came up in a petition in 1847, from the English Peace Society to
Parliament.

The next year this subject was discussed in
the Peace Congress at Brussels.

A few months later, Cobden brought forward
in the House of Commons an address to the
Government, with the request that the Minister
of Foreign Affairs should be charged to invite
foreign powers to enter into treaties with this

object. The proposal was in the beginning received with astonishment and scorn; but called forth later an earnest and important debate.

About six years later, HENRY RICHARD drew the attention of many influential members of the American Congress to the relations which were felt to be favourable for trying to arrange a treaty of arbitration between Great Britain and the United States. American statesmen, less bound by the old traditions of European diplomacy would, it was thought, be able with greater freedom to attempt such a novelty. The replies to this application were very favourable and encouraging, and in various ways since then attempts have been made to realize the idea.

IN MANY PARLIAMENTS from time to time propositions in this direction have been brought forward and approved.

On July 8th, 1873, Henry Richard brought before the English Parliament a proposition requesting the Government to invite negotiation with foreign powers for creating a universal and well-established international system of arbitration. The then Prime Minister,

Gladstone, expressed himself as favourable to the proposal, but advised its being withdrawn. Richard, nevertheless, persisted that it should be dealt with, and obtained the remarkable result, that it was carried with a majority of ten.

This example was followed by the ITALIAN CHAMBER OF DEPUTIES, Nov. 24th of the same year; and again on July 12th, 1890;[1] by the STATES GENERAL OF HOLLAND, Nov. 27th, 1874; by the BELGIAN CHAMBER OF REPRESENTATIVES, Dec. 19th, 1875; and shortly after by the SENATE of the United States of America, and CONGRESS also, June 17th, 1874; and April 4th, 1890.

The last-named resolution of Congress had been accepted by the Senate, Feb. 15th of the same year, being recommended by the Committee on Foreign Affairs, and runs thus :—

The President be, and is hereby requested to invite from time to time, as fit occasions may arise, negotiations with any government with which the United States has or may have diplomatic relations, to the end that any difficulties or disputes arising between them, which cannot be adjusted

---

[1] On a motion by Ruggiero Bonghi, supported by Crispi in a speech in which he said that the future depended upon a European tribunal of arbitration.

by diplomatic agency, may be referred to arbitration, and
be peaceably adjusted by such means.

On May 9th, 1890, Don Arturo de Marcoartu
moved in the SPANISH SENATE that the Spanish
Government should enter into relations with
other European powers to bring about a permanent tribunal of arbitration in Europe.   In
the first place, the mover proposed that the
states should come to an agreement upon a
general truce for five years.   In that interval
a congress of emissaries from all the European
Governments and Parliaments should be called
together.   The business of the congress should
be to work out a code of international law.
The proposition was urged, especially with
regard to the necessity of finding a reasonable
solution of the great social question, since all
effort in that direction appears to be hopeless
so long as the savings of the nations are
swallowed up by military expenditure.   The
Minister of Foreign Affairs requested the
Senate to take the proposition into serious
consideration, and on June 14th the Senate
resolved to authorize the Government to enter
into negotiations with foreign powers for the
object indicated.

Neither are the Scandinavian Parliaments unaffected by this movement.

As far back as 1869 the question of arbitration was mooted in the SWEDISH PARLIAMENT by Jonas Jonassen. In 1874 he proposed in the second chamber that Parliament should submit to the King " that it would behove his majesty on all occasions that might present themselves to support the negotiations which foreign powers might open with Sweden or with each other with reference to the creation of a tribunal of arbitration for the solving of international disputes." The committee which dealt with the proposition advised its acceptance. The Lower House passed it, March 21st, by seventy-one votes against sixty-four ; but the Upper House rejected it.

The miserable dealing of the Parliament of 1890 with the question I shall have occasion to refer to further on.

In the same year, the question made surprising advance in NORWAY. On March 5th the Storting voted on the motion of Ullmann and many others, by eighty-nine votes against twenty-four, an address to the King, which begins thus :—

"The Storing hereby respectfully approaches your Majesty, with the request that your Majesty will make use of the authority given by the constitution in seeking to enter into agreements with foreign powers, for the settling by arbitration of disputes which may arise between Norway and those powers."

And concludes with these words :—

"In the full assurance that what the Storting here requests will be an unqualified benefit to our people, it is hereby submitted that your Majesty should take the necessary steps indicated."

A similar resolution was very near, being voted by the DANISH FOLKETING in 1875. The proposition as brought forward was, May 13th, unanimously recommended by the committee in charge, but on account of the dissolution of the House two days later, could not be acted upon.

Several years ago a petition was circulated in the various districts of Denmark, by which Parliament was urged to co-operate as early as possible in bringing about a permanent Scandinavian treaty of arbitration.

In such a treaty, binding in the first instance for thirty years, the petition affirms that the three northern kingdoms will have an efficient moral support when there is occasion to withstand the efforts of the great powers to entice or to threaten any of them to take part in war as allies on one side or the other. Such a treaty will, therefore, in great measure serve to preserve the neutrality of the northern kingdoms, and thereby their lasting independence.

This petition was dealt with in the Folketing, March 27th, 1888. After a short discussion, the following motion of F. Bajer was passed by fifty votes against sixteen.

"Since the Folketing agrees with the wish expressed in the petition, provided it is shared by the other States without whom it cannot be carried out, the House passes on to the order of the day."

In his little paper : *On the Prevention of War by Arbitration*, F. Bajer writes :

"It may certainly be granted, that a little State like Denmark cannot well work at the creation of a European tribunal of arbitration, so far as that means setting itself at the head of a movement for inviting the other European States to a Congress by which its creation shall be adopted.

"But a little State like Denmark can always do something in the direction of arbitration between States. It can bring the matter a practical step forward by applying first to the other small States, especially to the neighbour States of Sweden and Norway, and proposing to them that mutual disputes shall in future, as far as possible, be settled by arbitration when other means have failed. The relations

between the three northern kingdoms are indeed now so
friendly that a war between them can hardly be thought of
for a moment. But—as was said in confirmation of the
resolution in the first northern Peace Meeting, respecting a
permanent arbitration treaty between the three kingdoms—
they have carried on many bloody internecine wars, which
have only benefited their powerful neighbours, but have
been in the highest degree injurious to themselves; and
the possibility of war between the three northern kingdoms is not excluded so long as they are not simultaneously
neutralized, or in some other way engaged to carry out a
common foreign policy. It is no longer ago than 1873
that the so-called "pilots' war" in Oeresund caused much
bad blood among relatives on both sides of the sound.
That that was settled authoritatively by the mutual declaration of the 14th of August is due to circumstances on whose
continuance for the future it is not possible to reckon.
Had a strained relation at the same time obtained between
one or more of the great powers within or without the
Baltic ports, and had these endeavoured to sow discord
between the coast powers, that they might fish in the
troubled waters, and feather their own nests by getting
these small states as their allies; and if one power had got
Denmark, but its enemy got Sweden-Norway as an ally
—a new northern fratricidal war would have broken out.
Even if such a future possibility cannot be entirely eradicated by a mutual arbitration treaty amongst the northern
nations, a new guarantee for peace would be secured."
(Bluntschli's expression.) "For the small northern kingdoms would by such a treaty acquire an excellent moral
support when it came to withstanding the attempt of
the great powers to entice or threaten them into taking part
in wars as their allies. Such a participation is always a

dangerous game, because, as history shows, the small States lose rather than gain. The small States are used as counters for the great ones to play with."

At this point we may remark, that as far back as 1848, the same year that the Peace Congress was held in Brussels, Feb. 2nd, a treaty (the Guadaloupe-Hidalgo Treaty) was concluded between the United States of America and Mexico, containing a clause that a committee of arbitration shall settle, not only such differences as may arise directly concerning that treaty, but also shall, as the highest authority, adjudicate as far as possible all disputes which may arise between the high contracting States.[1]

SWITZERLAND concluded, July 20th, 1864, a similar treaty with the HAWAIAN ISLANDS, and on October 30th with SAN SALVADOR.[2]

Siam, whose monarch has given many proofs of sympathy for Oskar II., concluded a similar treaty, May 18th, 1868, with the UNITED KINGDOMS, and also with BELGIUM, Aug. 29th of the

[1] See Martens' "Nouveau recueil général," xiv. p. 32 (art xxi.), and Calvo, " Droit International," II., § 1499.
[2] According to a Manuscript by President Louis Ruchonnet, addressed to F. Bajer.

same year.[1] The CENTRAL and SOUTH AMERICAN
REPUBLICS, HONDURAS, and THE UNITED
STATES OF COLOMBIA did the same when on
April 10th, 1882, they signed an arbitration
treaty between themselves.[2]

Since that time this vigorous idea has grown
into the CENTRAL AND SOUTH AMERICAN ARBI-
TRATION LEAGUE, and is now making good way
towards being applied to the whole of America.

The question now is, whether the VALUE OF
PEACE TREATIES, in general or in particular,
which are established between mutually distant
small States can be estimated as highly as the
good intention of their creation, which is
habitually acknowledged to be good? Are

---

[1] See "Svensk förfaltningssamling," 1869, No. 74, page
26, and "Lois Belges," 1869, No. 36, § 24. In the
Swedish-Siamese treaty, art. 25, it is stated: "Should any
disagreement arise between the contracting parties which
cannot be arranged by friendly diplomatic negotiation or
correspondence, the question shall be referred for solution
to a friendly neutral power, mutually chosen, whose decision
the contracting powers shall accept as final. Similar agreements are to be concluded between Italy and Switzerland,
Spain and Uruguay, Spain and Hawaii, and between France
and Ecuador.

[2] The Treaty is given word for word in the *Herald of
Peace*, July, 1883.

they something to be depended upon ? Will
they be carried into effect ?

That depends in the first place upon what
is meant by peace treaties.

If reference is made to certain international
settlements which the conquered, with hatred
in their hearts, bleeding, upon their knees
were FORCED to accept, we may at once grant
that they imply no security for peace, but, on
the contrary, are a fresh source of warlike
complications.

Thus, for example, the conclusion of peace
which France was FORCED to sign at Versailles,
Feb. 26th, 1871, and by which Alsace-Lorraine
was torn from France, became a volcano which
now for nineteen years has held the nations in
suspense and unrest, and still threatens to ruin
Europe.

Neither would it be advisable to set much
store on such obligations as the Western
Powers undertook in the agreement which
goes by the name of the NOVEMBER TREATY,
to help us to defend the northern part of our
peninsula against Russia ; because a guaranteed neutrality implies in reality more danger
than safety, if the guarantee is not mutual ; that

is, in this instance, if our eastern neighbour is
not included in the guarantee; which is so far
from being the case that the treaty, on the contrary, is a source of menace and distrust to him. [1]

With respect to certain treaties of alliance,
whose object is to collect THE GREATEST POS-
SIBLE NUMBER OF BAYONETS as a mutual security
against other powers, who, on their side, seek
to protect themselves by uniting their forces,
nobody can see in them anything else than a
guarantee for an armed peace, which, by the
necessity of its nature, leads to war.

If, on the contrary, by peace treaties are
meant such international contracts as are NOT
WRITTEN IN BLOOD; such as relate to trade and
commerce, industry, art, science and so on, it
would be in vain to seek for a single instance

[1] In this treaty, which was concluded at Stockholm,
Nov. 21st, 1855, the King of Norway and Sweden
bound himself not to resign to Russia, or to barter with
her, or otherwise allow her to possess, any portion of the
territory of the united kingdoms, nor to grant to Russia
right of pasture or fishery, or any similar rights, either on
the coast of Norway or Sweden. Any Russian proposal
which might be made under this head must be made
directly to France or England, who then by sea and land
must support us by their military power. A glorious contrast to the declaration of neutrality, Dec. 15th, 1853!

of the breach of contract, either on the side of the weaker or the stronger.

Neither can any example in our time be pointed to of open violation of the rights of a small country in its quality of an independent State, as long as these rights have stood under the mutual guarantee of the great powers,

As evidence to the contrary, the London treaty of May 8th, 1853, has been adduced, which was intended to secure Denmark's neutrality; the Treaty of Paris, April 14th, 1856, respecting the Black Sea; and the fifth article of the Peace of Prague in 1866. But here the fault lies in a misunderstanding.

What the Treaty of London established was not the indivisibility of Denmark, but of the Dano-German monarchy. The German territory was to be fast linked to the Danish. This was admitted, as a principle, by the treaty to be fitting and right, but the treaty contained no trace of stipulations as to guarantee.

With respect to Russia's breach of treaty of the stipulations as to her banishment from the Black Sea as a military power,[1] it must be

---

[1] Conquered Russia had to bind herself, at the conclusion of peace, not to keep war ships in the Black Sea, not to have

remembered that the representatives of the
powers, and of Russia also, on January 17th,
1871, signed a protocol, whereby it was settled
as an essential axiom in international law, that
no power can absolve itself from the obligations which are entered into by treaty without
the consent of the contracting parties. Therefore Russia openly acknowledged that her
declaration of not choosing to abide by the
injunctions stipulated for in the Treaty of Paris
respecting the Black Sea, was precipitate,
and that, consequently, the treaty was per-
manently in force until it was formally abro-
gated. This took place in the new treaty of
March 3rd, of the same year. Besides, here
comes in what was said above about the value
of such treaties as are concluded after brute
force has determined the issue. And this not
only was the case in the Black Sea stipulations,
but also with respect to the unfulfilled promises
of article 5 of the Treaty of Prague, whereby
the Danish people was to be given the opportunity for a plebiscite in determining upon their

any haven for war ships on her coasts. Stipulations which
were perceived by all thinking men at the time to be untenable in the long run.

reunion with Denmark. As to the peace
treaties between the lesser States, which certainly have important trade relations one with
another, but which, on account of their mutually
distant position, cannot reasonably be expected
to go to war with each other, it is true that
one cannot in general attribute any special
importance to them. Nothing is gained by
over-estimating their value. But they deserve
to be brought forward as enrichments of international law and guide-posts for other States.
And that the small States need not wait until
the great ones are ready to unite appears just
as much in accordance with the nature of the
case as with the interests of their own well-
being.

Calvo, undeniably the first authority in these
matters, emphasizes as a significant fact, that
no single example can be pointed to in which
States, after their mutual disputes have been
referred to the consideration or judgment of
arbitrators, have sought to *withdraw from
the operation* of the decision. And according
to Henry Richard and other authorities, by
allowing international questions to be settled
by arbitration, at least in sixty-seven instances,

disputes of a menacing character have been averted.

I shall not here give a detailed account of all these instances, but only with the greatest conciseness refer to some of them.

In 1794 a contest between England and the United States of America respecting St. Croix river was settled by arbitration; in 1803 France was in the same way condemned to pay 18 million francs to the United States of America for unlawful seizure of vessels; in 1818 a threatening dispute between Spain and the United States of America was settled by arbitration, and a contention between these and England was arranged by the Emperor of Russia, who was chosen as arbitrator, etc.

The best known of such disputes was the so-called Alabama question, which threatened a desolating world-war. This affair sprang out of the North American civil war 1861–65. The Southern States had privateers built in England, among which the *Alabama* especially wrought great mischief to the Northerners. The Government of the Union considered that England had broken her neutrality in allowing the equipment of the privateer, and requested compensation.

A bitter feeling grew up and war appeared inevitable. But on January 24th, 1869, an agreement was happily entered into, which, with fresh negotiations, led to the Washington treaty, May 8th, 1871. In harmony with this the dispute was referred for settlement to a Court of Arbitration consisting of five members, of which England and the United States each chose one, and the neutral states of Italy, Switzerland, and Brazil, likewise each chose one. These five met on December 15th, 1871, as a tribunal of arbitration, at Geneva, and delivered their judgment on September 14th following (four votes against England's one), that the English Government had made a breach in its duty as a neutral power with respect to some of the privateers under consideration, and therefore England would have to pay an indemnity of $15\frac{1}{2}$ million dollars to the United States.[1]

England bowed to the award and fulfilled her duty.

---

[1] £3,196,874 were received by Sec. Fish, Sept. 9th, 1873. See Haydn's "Dictionary of Dates."

In the same way the powerful insular kingdom voluntarily submitted to settlement in
the weary contention regarding the possession
of Delagoa Bay and the surrounding region
on the east coast of Africa. The dispute was
entrusted for settlement, in 1874, to the
President of the French Republic, MacMahon,
and he decided in July, 1875, in favour of
Portugal. That the new contention between
these two States, which for some time now
has excited an inflammable spirit, not only in
Portugal, but in other countries as well, will
be arranged in the same friendly manner, there
is but little doubt.

The claim of Portugal is much older than
that of England. Its special ground is the dis-
covery of the coast which was made by Portuguese mariners three hundred years ago. The
Portuguese urge, that since the coast is theirs,
they have a right to go as far inland as they
choose and place the country thus entered
under their dominion. They say further, that
they have made a treaty with a native ruler
over a kingdom which stretches far inland, and
that ruined fortresses are still to be found which
show that they once had this distant region in

possession. To this assertion Lord Salisbury answers, that where ruined fortresses are found they only testify to fallen dominion. The English Government could not recognise Portugal's construction of the contested question; according to that construction the question would virtually turn upon the possession of Shireland and Mashonaland (the inland country north and south of the Zambesi). It denied Portugal's claim to this territory as so entirely groundless that it could not enter into such a question; but has on the other hand made a peremptory claim, arising from Portugal's violence towards the natives who are under England's protection, for dishonour to the English flag, and for other international offences, etc.

The right of possession of the regions in question can no longer be regarded as doubtful, since Portugal had set aside the general international axiom, that the claim for possession according to colonial usage can only be held valid when colonization is actually carried out to the furtherance of civilization and public safety. Portugal's assertion that the signatories of the Congo Act would be the right adjudicators of the question was denied, upon the

ground that Portugal had delayed to make her
claim valid when Nyassaland was declared to belong to the sphere of England's interests. On
July 1st, 1889, the Under-secretary, Sir James
Fergusson, in the Lower House, explained that
the Portuguese Government had been informed
that they would be held answerable for all loss
which Englishmen might suffer by the annulling
of the Delagoa railway convention. The same
day Lord Salisbury informed the Upper House
that the English Government would send three
war-ships to Delagoa Bay, to be ready in case of
need. Portugal's conduct was, in his opinion,
unjustifiable.

Then came the noble lord's ultimatum, with
the demand that Portugal should recall all
Portuguese officers and troops from the territory which stands under the sovereignty of
England or lies within the sphere of England's
interests, and give an answer within twenty-
four hours ; otherwise England would be compelled to break off her relations with Portugal.
This threatening manner of procedure, by which
a weaker nation was humbled by superior
power, roused bad blood in Portugal and was
sharply censured in many parts of Europe ; yes,

even in England, and in Parliament, in the press, and at many great public meetings. At one of these meetings, composed of 700 workmen delegates from various parts of England and 130 Members of Parliament, in quality of vice-presidents, it was unanimously resolved to protest against Lord Salisbury's conduct as at variance with the dignity of the British nation; and to request that the dispute should be settled by arbitration—so much the rather, as the more certain one is of being in the right, the more confidently can one's cause be placed in the hands of an impartial tribunal. Later on the English Government, together with the North American virtually resolved on this expedient for solving the difficulties relating to Delagoa Bay. Portugal made difficulties and delays, but at length declared herself willing to enter into a proposal for arbitration.[1] All three States were now united in asking the Government of Switzerland to choose three of her most distinguished jurist officials as arbitration judges.

At the time when the first Anglo-Portuguese contest was settled by the President of the French Republic there occurred a second ex-

[1] *The Arbitrator*, 1890, April.

ample of both importance and interest.   For
many years there had been a menacing boundary dispute between Italy and Switzerland, just
a little seed of quarrel, such as formerly always
broke out into bloody strife, since according
to the traditions of national honour not an inch
of a patch of ground must be given up except
at the sword's point.   But the two kingdoms
decided to commend the case to an arbitrator,
viz., the United States minister in Rome, P.
Marsh, who, after a careful study of the claims of
the contending parties, declared judgment in favour of Italy, and so the contention was adjusted.

TWO DANGEROUS DISPUTES, which in 1874–75
and 1880 threatened an outbreak of war between CHINA and JAPAN, but were happily solved
by arbitration, might be named, but for fear of
being prolix I dare not go more particularly
into them, instructive as they are.

The first arose as a result of a murder of
some Japanese on the island of Formosa, and
was settled by the English minister in Pekin,
who was chosen by both parties as arbitrator,
who decided that China should give Japan in
redress a large sum of money, which was done.[1]

[1] The Japanese Government demanded redress, which was

The second of these disputes concerned the sovereignty of the Liu Kiu Islands, and was

at first refused by China. This led to a stormy corre-spondence, which at last became so bitter that both sides prepared for war. The Japanese troops had already taken possession of Formosa. During this dangerous juncture, the British minister in Pekin, Sir Thomas Wade, offered to mediate as an arbiter. The offer was accepted, and led to an agreement between the Chinese Government and the Japanese ambassador in Pekin, by which China was to pay Japan 500,000 taels, and the Japanese troops were to evacuate Formosa. When Lord Derby, who was at that time Foreign Secretary of Great Britain, received a telegram from Sir Thomas Wade respecting this happy result, he answered him : "It is a great pleasure to me to present to you the expression of the high esteem with which her Majesty's Government regards you for the service you have rendered in thus peaceably adjusting a dispute which other-wise might have had unhappy consequences, especially to the two countries concerned, but also for the interests of Great Britain and other parties to treaties." Sir Harry Parkes, the English minister in Japan, wrote to Lord Derby, that the Mikado, the Emperor of that land, had invited him to an interview for the purpose of expressing his satisfaction at the result, and through him to present his warm thanks for his brave and efficient service. The Japanese minister in London also called upon Lord Derby and expressed the thanks of his Government to Mr. Wade. "He could assure me," said Lord Derby, when he repeated the words of his excellency, "that the service which has thus been rendered will remain in grateful remembrance among his country-men."

D

adjusted by a compromise brought about by
ex-president Grant, who in a conversation with
the Chinese Minister uttered these memorable
words : " An arbitration between two nations
will never satisfy both nations alike ; but it
always satisfies the conscience of humanity." [1]

Not to be tedious, I pass over here many
other remarkable instances in which war and
lesser misfortunes have been averted by arbi-

[1] This dispute had assumed quite a serious and menacing character when the ex-president Grant, on his journey
round the world, came to China. When his arrival became known, the Chinese prince, Kung, submitted to him
that he should use his great influence in mediating between
the two countries. A specially interesting conversation
followed : "We have," said Prince Kung, "studied international law as it is set forth by English and American
authors, whose works are translated into Chinese. If any
value is to be set upon principles of international right, as set
forth by the authors of your nation, the doing away with the
independence of the Liu Kiu Islands is an injustice." Grant
reminded him that he was there only as a private individual,
but added, "It would be a true joy to me if my advice or
efforts could be the means of preserving peace, especially
between two nations for whom I cherish such interest as
for China and Japan." Immediately afterwards he returned
to Tokio, the capital of Japan, called upon the Emperor and
his Minister, and advocated a peaceable settlement of the
dispute. He wrote to Prince Kung the result of his mediation, and produced a scheme for a Court of Arbitration.

tration ; and will now name further only some of the latest date.

In 1887 a lengthened dispute about boundaries between CHILI and the ARGENTINE REPUBLIC was adjusted by arbitration, through the mediation of the United States Ministers in the two countries. After a complete and precise fixing of the boundary line, an agreement was added : That the Straits of Magellan shall for ever be neutralized ; free passage shall be secured to ships of all nations, and the erection of forts or other military works on either of its shores shall be forbidden.

Fresh in the memory is the passionate quarrel between SPAIN and GERMANY about the CAROLINE ISLANDS. That was submitted, on Prince Bismarck's proposal, to Pope Leo XIII. for settlement, and was adjusted by him.

Most people now living remember the AFGHANISTAN BOUNDARY question, which was happily solved by the friendliness on both sides of the RUSSIAN AND ENGLISH Governments. The whole world followed for a while that dispute with anxiety and disquietude. The press unhappily, as usual, employed its influence in stirring up the national passions in both countries. But before it had gone too far, fortunately the feelings were quieted by the public being reminded that both England and Russia had taken part in the resolution of the Paris Congress, which declared that when any serious dispute arose between any of the contracting powers, it should be referred to the mediation of a friendly power. Upon this ground the English Government proposed to the Russian that the "dispute should be referred to the ruler of a friendly State, to be adjusted in a manner consistent with the dignity of both lands." This proposal was accepted, but did not come into practice. It was not needed. The Afghanistan boundary commission itself carried out its duties to a successful issue.

Still later many smaller INTERNATIONAL DISPUTES have been solved by arbitration; for instance :—

Between ITALY and COLOMBIA in South America, respecting Italian subjects who had suffered loss through the last revolution in Colombia, in which Spain as arbitrator decided in favour of Italy.

Between BRAZIL and ARGENTINA respecting

their boundaries, a dispute in which both parties appealed for a settlement to the President of the United States of America, and which was adjusted by him.

Between the UNITED STATES of North America and DENMARK, in which the latter was, by the chosen arbitrator, the English Ambassador at Athens, Sir Edward Monson, after long delay freed from the obligation to pay compensation to the Americans, because the Danish authorities had fired at an American ship which in 1854 was escaping out of the harbour of St. Thomas, and which was suspected of carrying supplies to Venezuela, at that time in insurrection.

In conclusion it can be urged,—

That FRANCE and HOLLAND agreed to have the boundary between their possessions in Guiana determined by arbitration.[1]

---

[1] At the Peace of Utrecht, 1713, it was decided that the course of the river Maronis was the boundary. But that river divides itself into two branches which embrace a large tract of land, almost a fifth part of French Guiana. Neither France nor Holland had claimed that land until gold beds were discovered there, and it had to be decided which of the two arms of the river was to be considered as the Maronis, and which as a tributary.

That the international committee which met in Washington to arrange the impending fishery question between GREAT BRITAIN, CANADA and the UNITED STATES, decided to recommend the creation of a permanent tribunal of arbitration for adjusting future disputes respecting these relations ; also

That the council of the Swiss Confederation, at the combined request of PORTUGAL and of the CONGO STATE Government has undertaken to arbitrate the possible disputes which may arise respecting the regulation of boundaries amongst their African territories.

Besides these and other instances which I am acquainted with, many others have certainly taken place, though attracting less attention.

The idea of arbitration goes peacefully and quietly forward, and the world therefore takes little notice of it.

It is quite otherwise with the crash of war, whose external show of greatness and glory, and whose inward hatred and crime, are desolating the happiness of the nations and are accompanied by distress and gloom.

The one is a fearful hurricane which rends the mountains and breaks in pieces the rocks.

The other is the still small voice, mightier than the devastating storm, since it speaks to us in the name of everlasting righteousness, because it is the voice of God.

NEUTRALITY.

SIDE by side with the idea of arbitration, another pacific idea, already powerful, is pressing forward, and growing into an International Law, namely, the Law of Neutrality.

He is neutral, who neither takes part for, nor against, in a dispute. Neutrality is the impartial position which is not associated with either party. The State is called neutral which neither takes part in a war itself, nor in time of war sides with any of the warring parties.

In ancient times neutrality was not understood as a national right. Neither the Greek nor the Latin language has any word to express the idea. In the days when Roman policy was seeking to drag all the nations of the earth into its net, the Romans saw in other peoples only tributaries who had been subdued by their armies, subject nations who had submitted to the Roman yoke, allies who were compelled to join in their policy of conquest, or lastly enemies, who sooner or later would have to bow before their victorious legions. Neutral States there were none.

The centuries immediately following the dissolution of the Western Roman Empire were filled with constant strife. This continued long before the refining power which exists in the heart of Christianity began to show itself in the foreign relations of States.

The foundations of modern Europe were laid in war.

During the Crusades the whole of our continent was under arms. The struggle against the "infidel" was not simply a contest between one State and another, it was also a contest between Christian Europe and Mohammedan Asia. To be neutral in such a struggle would, according to the judgment of the time, have been equivalent to denying the faith. Within the European States, feudalism exerted no less a hindrance to the embodiment of the principle of neutrality. It would have been thought the gravest crime to loosen the bond of military service which compelled vassals to support with arms the cause of their feudal lords. It was only with the close of the age of feudalism, when Europe began to separate into three or

four great monarchies, that neutrality in politics
became a means of preserving the balance.

In later times increasing COMMUNICATION and
TRADE have above all contributed to the development of neutral laws. Without the
sanction of these, a naval war between two
great nations would have made any maritime
trade all but impossible. Down to the close of
the last century, however, neutral rights were
dependent either on national statutes or on
special treaties concluded between one State
and another. The law only gained certain
international importance towards the close of
the eighteenth century through the NEUTRAL
ALLIANCES which from time to time were con-
tracted between States.

In the period between 1780 and 1856 the
subject gained an entrance by degrees among
all maritime nations except England, who, independent of it, and always relying on her own
strength, continuously sought to maintain unlimited domination at sea.

In 1854–56 begins, so far as neutrality is
concerned, a new era of international law.

From this time the opposition which England raised to the practical application of neu-

trality in naval war may be regarded as having broken down. On the 30th of March, 1854, the French Minister of Foreign Affairs, Drouyn de Lhuys, published a communication, including, amongst other things, that the neutral flag during the then begun (Crimean) war, should be regarded as a protection for all neutral and hostile private property, except contraband of war. The same day the English Government gave forth in the *London Gazette* a similar declaration, and on April 19th of the same year the Russian Government notified in the *Official Gazette* of St. Petersburg that Russia would, during that war, act upon the same rules as the Allied powers.

The provisions, which thus the Western powers on one side, and Russia on the other, believed themselves bound to observe towards neutral states, were at the Peace of Paris, 1856, solemnly ratified as International Law in force for all time. The principles which the plenipotentiary signatories of the Peace Treaty of Paris agreed upon in a proclamation of April 16th, 1856, are as follows :—

1. Privateering is and shall be abolished.
2. The neutral flag shall protect property

belonging to the enemy, with the exception of contraband of war. 3. Neutral goods, except contraband of war, may not be seized under the enemy's flag. 4. Blockades in order to be obligatory must be fully effectual; that is, shall be maintained with a strength really sufficient to prevent approach to the enemy's coast.

The Governments which signed the treaty bound themselves also, in this proclamation, to communicate the resolutions to the States which were not called to take part in the Paris Conference, and to invite them to agree in these decisions. All the European States except Spain, and a number of powers outside Europe, declared themselves ready to carry out in practice the entire resolutions of the proclamation.

Many wars since then have shaken Europe; but under all these misfortunes the warring States have not only conscientiously observed the principles laid down in 1856, but they have gone further, in certain points, in applying them, than they by it were bound to do. Thus the Austrian Government issued an order, during the war with France and Sardinia, with respect to maritime national law, in many points far beyond what hostile or neutral powers had any ground for requesting. The Imperial decree not only charged its military and civil officers to follow strictly the injunctions of the proclamation, but Sardinian and French vessels, which lay moored in Austrian waters, were also to be permitted to load freight and proceed to foreign seas, on condition that they took on board no contraband of war or prohibited goods of any description. Immediately on the outbreak of war, the same principles were adopted by France and Sardinia. These States, however, went a step further than Austria, inasmuch as they unreservedly declared that they would not regard coal as a contraband of war.

During the Dano-German War, in 1864, and the war between Austria and Prussia and Italy, in 1866, the international principles of maritime law received a similarly wide interpretation.

During the North American Civil War important questions came up, which more or less affected the principle of neutrality. The question, which became one of the greatest importance, arose in respect of the injury which

the commerce and navigation of the Union
suffered during the war from various privateers
which were built in England on the Southerners'
account.

The ALABAMA QUESTION took its name from
the privateer which went out from Liverpool
and occasioned the greatest devastation while
the war lasted. Although the executive of the
Union at Washington duly directed the attention of the English Government to the fact
that allowing the pirate to leave the English
port would be equivalent to a breach of the
peace, yet the Government took no measures
to prevent the vessel leaving. The American
Government, who with reason regarded this
omission as a violation of the laws of neutrality,
claimed from England full compensation for
the property which had been destroyed in the
course of the civil war by the Southern privateer
which came from an English port. I have previously given more particularly the constitution
and functions of the Court of Arbitration appointed to settle the threatening dispute which
arose on this occasion. The arbitration award
had to be adjudicated in accordance with the
three following fundamental principles of international law :—

A neutral Government is bound :—

1. To guard assiduously against any vessel being armed or equipped in its ports, which there is reason to believe would be employed for warlike purposes against a peaceful power, and with equal assiduity to prevent any vessel designed for privateering, or other hostility, from leaving the domain of the neutral State :

2. Not to allow any belligerent power to make use of its ports or harbours as the basis of its operations, or for strengthening or repairing its military strength, or for enlisting :

3. To use every care within its ports and harbours and over all persons within its domain, to prevent any violation of the obligations named.

The contracting parties to this treaty agreed to hold themselves responsible for the future, and to bring them before the notice of other Maritime powers, with the recommendation that they also should enter into them.

The historical facts here produced show that the mutual interest nations have in the inviolability of the seas has effectually contributed to the development of an accepted international law.

When the necessity of making the principles
of neutrality binding at sea was once understood, it was not long before the value of adopting them on land became apparent.

In the documents, for instance, by which Belgium, Switzerland and Luxemburg are neutralized, it is distinctly stated that the permanent
neutrality of these States is in full accord with
the true interests of European policy.

According to the actual modern law of
nations, there is a permanent neutrality guaranteed by international deeds of law and treaties,
and one occasionally resting upon free decisions.[1]

As instances of permanent and guaranteed
neutrality, we have : The NEUTRALIZATION OF

---

[1] This and the following regulations are taken from
Bluntschli's "Das moderne Völkerrecht der civilizirten
Staatens," Nordlingen, 1872. Some of the treaty provisions
and questions are grounded upon " Recueil des traités, con-
ventions," etc., par Ch. de Martens and F de Cussy, Leipzig,
1846, and " Archives diplomatiques : "
—Since practical abstaining from war is the natural assump-
tion of neutrality, a neutral State is bound not to assist any
belligerent power in warlike purposes.
—A neutral State may not supply a belligerent power with
weapons or other war material.
—If private persons furnish belligerent powers with war
material as articles of commerce, they assuredly run the risk

SWITZERLAND. Ever since the unhappy Italian war in the beginning of the sixteenth century, the Swiss Confederation has endeavoured to assure to the country the security which neutrality gives.

This neutrality was recognised and guaranteed by the great European powers at the Congress of Vienna in 1815 (art. 84 and 92), and later was further solemnly confirmed by a special act of the powers at Paris, Nov. 20th of the same year, in which it was stated :

of confiscation by the contending parties of such articles, as contraband of war ; but the neutral *State* is not to be regarded as having violated its neutrality by tolerating trade in contraband of war.

—Permission freely to purchase food even upon account of a belligerent power is not regarded as a serious concession towards that State, provided that the permission is general, applying alike to both parties.

—A neutral State may not permit the war-ships of a belligerent power to run into its ports or (with any other object than to procure provisions, water, coal, etc.) to traverse its sounds, rivers and canals.

—Belligerent powers are bound fully to respect the right of peace of the neutral States, and to abstain from any invasion of their territories.

—Where a violation of neutral territory has taken place from ignorance of the boundary and not from evil intent, the neutral State shall immediately claim redress, compensation, and the adoption of measures necessary to prevent a similar mistake in future.

" The powers declare . . . by a permanent
act that the permanent neutrality and inviolability of Switzerland, as well as its independence of foreign influence, accords with the true
interests of European policy.[1]

THE NEUTRALIZATION OF BELGIUM. In
virtue of the Treaty of London, Nov. 15th,
1831 (art. vii.), further confirmed by the
powers April 19th, 1839, a permanent neutrality was awarded to Belgium.

This country, which for centuries had served
as a battle-ground for foreign powers, especially
for France and Germany, was hereby secured
against such dangers, and at the same time
the field for European warfare was materially
narrowed.

Article vii. of the London protocol runs
thus : " Belgium shall, within the boundaries
established in art. i. and iv., form an independent State. The kingdom is bound to observe
the same neutrality towards all States.[2]

During the Franco-German war 1870–1, the

[1] See in respect of this act, " Recueil des traités, conven-
tions," etc., Ch. de Martens and F. de Cussy, Part iii. p. 243
Leipzig, 1846.

[2] See Ch. de Martens and F. de Cussy, in the above-named
collection, Part iv. p. 575.

neutralization of Belgium was threatened with violation by France, and further guarantees were given in new protocols arranged by England.

THE NEUTRALIZATION OF THE ARCHDUCHY OF LUXEMBURG resulted from the London protocol of May 11th, 1867.

As an evidence of the power and importance in our day of entering into agreements of neutrality, the following may be adduced :—

During the Franco-German war, 1870–1, the Prussian Government complained to the guaranteeing powers of conduct at variance with neutrality on the part of Luxemburg, and threatened no longer to respect the neutrality of the Archduchy. (Despatch of Prince Bismarck, Dec. 3rd, 1870.)

In consequence of this, Count Beust, the Austrian chancellor, in an opinion given Dec. 22nd of the same year, remarked, that upon the ground of the principle of European guarantee, it belonged to the powers who had signed the document of neutralization, to inquire into and to settle whether a violation had taken place on the part of the neutral State, and not to one of the belligerent powers.[1]

[1] Respecting the correspondence on this question, see the remainder of " Archives diplomatiques," 1871–72.

Besides the States named, a permanent neutrality has been secured to the IONIAN ISLANDS
according to the treaties of London, 1863–64;
and also to the SAMOAN ISLANDS, in virtue
of the agreement between England, Germany,
and the United States of North America,
whereby, amongst other things, it was settled
that in case of any difference of opinion arising,
an appeal should be made to arbitration; and
that a supreme tribunal should be created with
a supreme judge, whom the King of Sweden
and Norway has been empowered to name.

———

One general advantage which neutralization
affords is the simplification with respect to
foreign policy thereby obtained.

The attitude of a neutralized State can be
reckoned on beforehand by all parties.

In proportion to its military importance and
position, a neutral country constitutes in many
ways a security to all the powers.

It is in close connection with neutralization
that in these days an ever-growing need is
becoming apparent to localize wars as much
as possible; that is, to confine them to those
who begin them.

As a result of the extraordinarily rapid development of world-wide trade and intercourse, and the consequent community of interests, a war between two States necessarily occasions more or less derangement to the rest.

In this increasing solidarity lies the surest guarantee that neutrality will be respected.

We may already be justified in drawing the conclusion that the security of neutral States will continually increase.

Supported upon these foundations of history and of international law, a discussion was raised on the neutralization of Sweden, in the First Chamber by Major C. A. Adelsköld, and by myself in the Second, in the hope thereby not only to oppose the King's bill for the extension of the war department, but also especially to open the way for a profitable solution of the tough, old, threadbare question of Defence.[1]

[1] Motion in the Second Chamber, No. 97.

Since the European States have settled into their present grouping, the material preponderance of the great powers over the smaller countries has more and more diminished the possibility of these defending their external liberty and independence by military power only.

There are States whose whole male population cannot

equal or barely exceed the number, which a great power can command for its fully equipped army.

In olden time, a small high-spirited people might with success fight against a greater and more powerful neighbour. In consequence of the weak organization, the feeble spirit of cohesion and the slightly developed art of war, it was then possible.

Now this condition is changed. As a rule we find that the military strength of a State is in direct proportion to its population and material wealth.

The consequence is that the smaller States have virtually ceased to be belligerent powers. Such examples as Germany's proceeding against Denmark in 1864, and England's against Egypt in 1882, or in general, when the stronger State only needs to consider how large a portion of its forces must be employed to accomplish its object, are not to be considered as wars, but as military executions.

As to our own country (Sweden), it certainly has, together with Norway, an advantage in its situation above other small powers. But it concerns us that we utilize this advantage with wisdom and at the right time. This is not to be done by turning Sweden into a military State, because even if we did so to the greatest possible extent, we should, if left to ourselves, not even so be in a condition to defend ourselves against our powerful neighbours.

In proportion as a nation exhausts its resources by military preparations, its ability lessens to cope with an overpowering enemy.

In our day, not only are great and well-disciplined hosts required for carrying on war, but great material riches are equally indispensable. The relation between a nation of four or five millions, and one of forty or fifty millions, is like that between the dwarfs and the giants.

It is easily understood that patriotic feelings may bewilder the judgment, and that our nation, with its brilliant war memories, can only with difficulty perceive this simple truth, and with reluctance accommodate itself to the changed condition which modern times have created.

Let us, however, realize that we are standing at the parting of the ways ; that we have before us the alternative, on the one hand, of a barren and ruinous militarism ; on the other, the seeking of our defence in a neutrality guaranteed by the united powers ; making it possible for us to get our defence adjusted, without any very great difficulty, and settled upon a footing so satisfactory.

The first-named alternative would, in our naturally poor land, excessively depress our natural vitality, and in a great degree prevent our progress as a cultured people keeping pace with greater and wealthier nations. The second would put us into a position to confine our military burdens within reasonable limits, and to expend the powers and resources of prosperity thus relieved, in means of promoting business, trade, science, and well-being of all kinds.

The clear-sighted friend of his country, who sees the population in ever-swelling numbers leaving their homes for a foreign shore, seeking a new fatherland, will surely not hesitate in his choice.

It will perhaps be said that such a choice does not now lie before us. There are two opinions about that. But in one thing we may all unite, namely, that a settled neutrality for Sweden is a thing to be aimed at. Here almost every interest of the fatherland converges.

But if such a neutralization is considered by many not a sufficient peace-protection under all circumstances, yet no one with reason can deny that it does form a security for our country against foreign powers.

Accepting this conclusion as correct, it follows that we should find some practicable means of realizing it ; and if hindrances do meet us, we shall, on nearer inspection, find that they are not great, but with hearty goodwill and perseverance may be overcome.

This is my conviction.

In drawing attention to the subjoined, I would further bring to mind that the seat of war in Europe is limited in the proportion in which the number of neutralized States grows, a condition of things which may little by little in an essential degree impede or prevent the outbreak of war ; that the peculiar situation of Sweden (greatly superior, for example, to Belgium or Switzerland) must naturally facilitate its neutralization ; that, lastly, the neutrality proposed does not stand in the way of arranging our own defence, but the rather, in case Parliament rejects his Majesty's army bill, adapts itself powerfully to contribute to a right solution of the *Defence question* ; and so much the more, as all suspicion that that old vexed question aims perhaps at something more and other than DEFENCE of the country would thereby disappear.

For this reason—and since we cannot expect that other powers should take the first step and offer us what we do not ask for—I respectfully propose :—

That Parliament shall in writing express to the king its desire that it might please his Majesty to initiate, amongst the states with which Sweden has diplomatic relations, negotiations for bringing about a permanent guaranteed[1] neutrality of Sweden, in harmony with the principles of modern international law.   K. P. ARNOLDSON.

STOCKHOLM, *February*, 1883.

[1] The word "guaranteed" was inserted in the motion contrary to the opinion of the committee.

This motion was supported by—

S. A. Hedlund,	J. Jonassen, Gullaboås,	Arvid Gumœlius,
Will. Farup,	C. J. Svensén,	J. Jonassen,
J. Andersson, Tenhuset,	A. Th. Wallenius,	Eric Olsson,
J. E. Ericsson, Ahlberga,	P. M. Larsson, Löa,	J. A. Ericsson,
Pehr Pehrsson,	P. G. Petersson,	Lars Nilsson,
F. F. Borg,	C. G. Otterborg.	

Before this resolution was brought into the Riksdag, I had read it to seventy members of the Riksdag, who unanimously accepted it, as did also, later on, in the main, a majority of the [Norwegian] Storting.[1] And as soon as the purport of the resolution became generally known through the press, there came in from popular meetings all over Sweden numerous

[1] Taken from the following communication :

At a meeting, March 31st, 1883, of the Association of members of the Storting, a document was presented, being a motion in the Second Chamber, No. 97, respecting the Neutralization of Sweden ; which document was sent to the president of the meeting by a Swedish M.P.

In consequence of this the following declaration and resolution was voted unanimously : Recognising that the neutralization of a single country is in the interest of universal peace ; that being secured from foreign attack by stronger nations, gives ability to use its own resources and develop its institutions, including its defence, according to

congratulatory addresses to Major Adelsköld
and myself.

But from its very commencement the proposition met with an unconquerable opposition
from those in power.

With great unanimity efforts were made in
this quarter to depreciate the value and the
historical importance of the principle of neutrality. All possible means were used with
this object, to touch the tenderest fibres of the
national feelings. It would be a disgrace to us,
it was said, to employ any other than military
power in asserting our primeval freedom. We
should thereby break off from our glorious
history, and draw a black line over its brilliant
warlike reminiscences. There were certainly
neutral countries to be found, but their neutrality was not the result of their own desire,

its special requirements ; that the condition and situation
of our country give equal opportunity for working for this
object, and facilities for its attainment ; and that the action
taken in the Swedish Rigsdag upon the question, seriously
calls our attention to it on the ground of the constitutional
relation between the kingdoms and their union in war and
in peace ; a committee is requested to take into consideration, how the question may be subjected to further attention.

A. QUAM, Secretary of the Association.

but proceeded from the great powers themselves. Should we then, they say further, be
the first people to take such a step? Would
it not be equivalent to begging peace of our
neighbour, and declaring ourselves incapable
before the whole world? The sensible thing
would be to further develop and strengthen our
army. The resolution was called a political
demonstration of indigence; a disgusting nihil-
ist plot, and so on. One member of the
Riksdag proposed that it should be consigned
to a committee charged with arranging for
sending beasts abroad. Scoffs came thick as
hail; and when it became known that the mover
in the *Second Chamber* was its author, the really
guilty one, he was branded as a universal
traitor,—just as the year before, when he raised
a peaceable question about extended liberty of
conscience.

In my defence of the resolution in the
Riksdag, I sought to anticipate all objections
to it which were worthy of notice.[1]

Amongst these I give special attention to the
following five :—

[1] Protocol of the Second Chamber, No 33, April 28th,
1883.

1. " The powers will not enter into the
   neutralization of Sweden.
2. " But if, contrary to expectation, they
   did, the safety of the country would
   gain nothing by it.
3. " On the contrary, our independence
   would be diminished by a guaranteed
   neutrality.
4. " Without lessening our military burdens
   for defence.
5. " The proposition is untimely."

With regard to the first objection, *viz.*, that
the powers would not enter upon Sweden's
neutralization, it appears to me that circumstances of great weight imply the contrary.

We may be quite sure that the powers will
first and foremost consult their own interests.
Scandinavia may be certainly regarded as
specially valuable as a base of military operations to any of the great Baltic and Western
States. But it would be quite a matter of
consideration, whether these powers would not
gain more by the reciprocal security of being all
alike cut off from this base, than by the doubtful
advantage of being possibly able to reckon upon
Scandinavia as an ally.

A neutralized Scandinavia would be a Switzerland among the seas ; a breakwater in the way between England and France on the one side, and Russia and Germany on the other. In case of a war between these great powers it would now be of considerable moment for any of them to get the powers along the coasts of the Sound and the Belts, upon its side. And how difficult it would be for the latter to preserve their neutrality during such a war, must be evident to everybody.

So the interests are seen to be equally great on all sides. It may therefore be deemed prudent to establish, in time, a permanent neutrality of the powers along the coast. Here, according to my view, lies a great problem for the foreign secretaries of the united kingdoms and Denmark.

My reason for speaking here of neutralizing the whole of Scandinavia is, that I am convinced that the brother-nations take entirely the same view as the Swedish. With respect to the general interests of European peace, the neutralization of Scandinavia would be more important than that of Switzerland and Belgium, because the interests of the great

powers are greater and more equally balanced
around the Scandinavian North than around
those two small continental States.

We have old friends in the Western powers;
we have gained a new friend in united
Germany; and by the neutralization of
Scandinavia we shall not only make friendship
with Russia, but Denmark will gain that of
Germany, perhaps causing the last-named
power to fulfil its duty to Denmark with
respect to North Sleswick, seeing that it need
no longer fear that its small neighbour would
ever be forced into an alliance with a powerful
enemy of Germany.

But it is not only the political interests of the
powers which would be advanced by the neutralization of Scandinavia.

In the course of the last ten years world-
wide traffic has made an unheard-of growth and
connecting links between nations have been
formed in many regions. As an example of the
effect of these we may mention that even thirty
years ago the normal freightage for corn was
50–60 shillings sterling per ton, from the Black
Sea to North Europe; but the freightage from
California and Australia to Europe, now, hardly

exceeds the half. A European war would exercise a paralyzing effect here. Every one who has any conception of the influence of the price of corn on, to speak broadly, the whole civilization of modern times, will easily understand this.

Before the century closes this development will have woven a net of common interest all over our continent, and necessarily called forth such a sensitiveness in the corporate body of Europe, that, for example, an injury in the foot of Italy may be said to cause pain right up to Norway.

The merchant fleet of Norway, alone, is indeed the third in rank of all the merchant fleets of the world. As is well known, the united kingdoms take an advanced place in the carrying trade by sea. According to what was told me by a distinguished merchant, the transport trade undertaken by Norwegian and Swedish ships between foreign countries is five times greater than that between home and foreign lands. Consequently, as the keen competition between steam and sailing vessels increases, the only country which can dispense with the service of our sailing vessels is

England, the great power upon which we may reckon always as an ally. Most of the remaining countries, on the other hand, require our merchant fleet.

Since, now, we could not of course defend our merchant service in a war, and other and greater nations may be jeopardized as much as we, it may be assumed that they would be willing, through the neutralization of Scandinavia, to secure its fleet against the eventualities of war.

If we add such interests as affect trade and credit, civilization and humanity, to the political interests, it appears that we may plead on grounds of strong probability that the great powers would be willing to guarantee our neutrality.

According to the second objection, the country would gain no security from a guaranteed neutrality, even if, contrary to expectation, such could be obtained.

Perfect safety cannot be attained here on earth by any system. This is as true for nations as for individuals; but I believe that a neutrality thus guaranteed would be a strong protection to our national independence, whilst in a not inconsiderable degree it would contribute to the preservation of peace, and gradually help to lessen the military burdens of all lands; consequently, and in the first place, of our own.

Treaties, it is said, are broken as easily as they are made. Even if it be true that this has occurred, it does not necessarily follow that it must continue to occur. New factors may come in making it more difficult to break engagements that have been entered into.

Experience shows that righteous laws have been transgressed, but no one would aver that they are therefore unnecessary. As the moral power of the law makes it possible to diminish the police force, so also treaties of neutrality make it possible to diminish the military forces.

Besides, our opponents ought to bring forward evidence that the rights of States at present neutralized have been violated. That they have been threatened is true, and it would have been a wonder if this had not happened under the lawless condition which has obtained among nations.

The idea of neutrality has, nevertheless, as I have tried to show by many examples, little by

F

little developed into a valid principle of justice ; and the growth continues. The neutralization of Scandinavia would bring it a great step forward, to the blessing both of ourselves and of other nations.

According to objections 3 and 4, a guaranteed neutrality would diminish our independence without contributing to lessen our burdens for defence.

The truth is, that international law as at present constituted does not permit another power to interfere under any pretext with the internal concerns of a neutral state, and therefore not with anything which affects its system of defence or its measures for preserving its neutrality. With these the neutral State, and it only, can deal.

As a proof of this being so, Luxemburg was neutralized in 1867 upon condition that the strong fortress bearing that name should be demolished. But this circumstance, imperative for the general peace of Europe, shows on the other hand that guaranteeing powers do not willingly impose upon a State any serious duty of fortifying itself in order to defend its rights. Nevertheless the powers found it needful to

make a supplementary clause to the protocol
by which the congress concluded the neutrality
of Luxemburg, whereby it was emphasized,
as a matter of course, that the article respecting
the destruction of the fortress of Luxemburg
did not imply any sort of limitation of the right
of the neutral State to maintain, or, if it chose,
to improve its own works of defence. Belgium
did indeed construct the great fortresses around
Antwerp long after the country was neutralized.

In reference to what one and another has
said about the value of the subject, nothing is
needed beyond the fact that neutral rights have,
even in its present position, been respected in
all essentials. That a neutral power must abstain from mixing itself up with the policy of
other powers cannot imply a greater limitation
of its right to self-regulation than that a guaranteeing power shall abstain from attacking
a neutralized State or from making military
alliance with it. There is certainly a limitation
for both parties, as far as is necessary for
adopting an intelligent union between States,
—a limitation of physical force and of love
of war.

The neutral State has not to submit to any

guardianship beyond what any man must do
and does, when he subjects his passions to the
control of a moral purpose.   -

Seeing that a guaranteeing State has no right
to interfere in our internal concerns, not even
in anything we think good for our defence, we
shall always be free to keep up a military force,
large or small. But a neutralized State is
obliged to disarm the troops of other belligerent
powers that may overstep its frontiers, just as
of course, under the lawless condition which
war is and which it entails, it has, according to
its ability, to protect its boundaries with arms.
But if this duty cannot exempt Switzerland and
Belgium from proportionately large war burdens
in time of peace, this would not at all in the
same degree affect the neutralization of the
Scandinavian peninsula, since there could never
be a question of disarming troops which had
overstepped its boundaries, but only of preventing the war-ships of a belligerent power
from entering Norwegian or Swedish seas, a
thing which, under the protection of a guaranteed neutrality, could not take place.

Respecting the fifth objection, which declares
that the proposition is untimely, I do not hesi-

tate to express my opinion that just now, during the truce which prevails, is the time to bring it forward. The need of a settled peace increases everywhere, and it is therefore probable that a proposition to the great powers respecting a guaranteed neutrality for the united kingdoms would meet with general sympathy in Europe.

On these and many other grounds I sought to maintain my proposition.

It was opposed by the Minister of Foreign Affairs, Baron Hochschild, amongst others, who declared that he could not possibly support it. He informed us that the whole of his colleagues in the Government took the same view of the subject as himself. He desired that the bill as well as the contingent appointment of a committee should be thrown out totally and entirely.

As the minister in this way has made the matter into a cabinet question, there could not well, under the present conditions, be any question of the adoption of the bill.

In spite of this, however, the request of the Foreign Minister was not complied with, seeing the Second Chamber adopted an amend-

ment after fifty-three members had voted for
the acceptance of the original bill.

By the amendment which was adopted, the
Chamber did not accept the grounds of the
committee's opinion — which the Foreign Secretary approved—but, in the hope that the
Government would spontaneously carry out the
chief object of the bill, accepted for the present the report of the committee that no address
be sent to the King on the subject.

By reason of this result in the Second
Chamber no action was taken in the First on
the matter.[1]

During the debate in the Second Chamber,
April 28, the Foreign Secretary remarked that
I must have overlooked the fact that the European powers had, ever since 1814, looked upon
the two kingdoms of the Scandinavian peninsula as a political unity in questions relating
to peace and war; why otherwise should I
propose from the first that the sister kingdom
should have the opportunity of expressing it-

---

[1] See on the dealing with the question in Parliament,
"Riksdagstrycket" 1883. Motion in the Second Chamber,
No. 97, pp. 1–8; First Chamber, protocol No. 33, pp. 3–4,
etc., etc.

self on a matter which concerned Norway equally with Sweden. This objection was without foundation.

During the drawn debate, March 3, I had already taken occasion to point out that it would not be seemly for one moving a resolution in the Swedish Riksdag to act as spokesman for Norway ; at the same time expressing my confidence that the Storting would meet us in a friendly manner, if the Riksdag approved the bill with respect to Sweden.[1]

---

[1] Mr. Arnoldson's speech ran thus :—

" The second speaker on the Right propounded certain difficulties, amongst others, one referring to Sweden's union with Norway. Since Sweden and Norway have the same foreign policy, and the initiative in this question comes from Sweden, the Union King ought certainly to be able to act freely in the common interest of the two kingdoms. In any case, it is probable, as Mr. Hedlund remarked, that if the Riksdag takes the first step it will not be long before the Storting comes to meet us. It was chiefly on the ground of courtesy that I did not undertake to speak for Norway too in the Riksdag. We know that the Norse—and it does them honour—are tenacious of their right of deciding for themselves. I do not think it would be seemly for the mover of such a resolution as this to make himself their spokesman in the Swedish Riksdag—not to mention the positive incorrectness of the proceeding. This is why I limited the matter to Sweden in my proposition."

That the neutralization ought to include no
only Norway, but Denmark too, seems to be
obvious.

A highly esteemed jurist, Count L. KAMA-
ROWSKY, professor of law at the University of
Moscow, puts it as a matter of great importance
in the interests of the world's peace that international seas and coasts should be neutralized.[1] This particularly affects Denmark in
connection with the other two Scandinavian
States. Such a neutralization, he says, will
lead to a disarmament in the Sound and Belts.
These great traffic-ways would then be acces-
sible for the merchant and war vessels of all
nations. They must not be fortified, but the
freedom of navigation would be watched over
by an international committee.

At the CONFERENCE at BERLIN in 1885, where
fifteen States were represented, just principles
were adopted for the navigation of the Congo
and the Niger. Free navigation and commerce
on these rivers was secured to the flags of all
nations. The same principle was likewise extended to their tributaries and lakes, together

[1] "Revue de droit international et de Legislation com-
parée," 1888, 2.

with canals and railroads which might in the future be constructed to get past the unnavigable portions of the Congo and Niger. Not even in time of war may the freedom of communication and commerce be interrupted. The transport of contraband of war alone is forbidden. An international commission takes care that all these international agreements are kept in force. This authority, composed of delegates from each of the States which took part in the Berlin Conference, is independent of the local authorities in Congo-land.

Now, every free people has naturally an independent right to arrange its own affairs as it chooses, upon condition that it grants the same right to every other State.

In consequence of this principle in international law, neutralization is applied in very varied ways according to the very varying conditions of those who have the benefit of it, and altogether in harmony with their wishes. Thus, for example, neutralization when it concerns a territory, consists not only in forbidding any warlike operation in the domain thus rendered inviolate, but involves a similar prohibition with respect to any marching or

countermarching of armies, or smaller detach-
ments, even of single officers or soldiers.

A canal or a strait may be so neutralized, on
the other hand, that all warlike operations are
forbidden in it, but nevertheless it is open for
passage through, yet upon condition that no
belligerent has a right, in passing through, to
land upon the shores of the neutralized region.

This is the kind of neutralization which
appears applicable to the Scandinavian seas.

One question which for a long time came up
constantly at the congresses of Peace Societies,
was the NEUTRALIZATION of the SUEZ CANAL,
until it became at last solved in practice. After
tedious negotiations, this burning question was
settled by an agreement between England and
France in the treaty of October 24, 1887, which
was later entered into by the other powers
interested ; and that important channel of communication became at all times inviolate.[1]

---

[1] The most important provisions of the treaty are the
following :—

Article 1. The Suez Canal shall always be free and open
whether in time of war or peace, for both merchant and war-
ships, whatever flag they carry. The treaty-powers therefore decide that the use of this canal shall not be limited

Upon the programme of the friends of peace questions have long been mooted respecting the neutralization of Elsass-Lothringen, and of the Balkan States, together with that of the Danube, Bosphorus, Sea of Marmora, Dardanelles, and their European coasts ; whereupon should follow the rendering inviolate of Constantinople ; as also of the Baltic, and as

either in time of peace or war. The canal can never be blockaded.

Article 4. No fortifications which can be used for military operations against the Suez Canal, may be erected at any point which would command or menace it. No points which command or menace its entrance or course may be occupied in a military sense.

Article 5 provides that, although the Suez Canal shall be open in war-time, no belligerent action shall take place in its vicinity or in its harbours, or within a distance from its area which shall be determined by the international committee that watches over the canal.

Article 6 is a continuation of the foregoing and runs thus : In time of war none of the belligerent powers are permitted to land, or to take on board, ammunition or other war material, either in the canal or in its harbours.

Article 8. The powers are not allowed to keep any warship in the waters of the canal. But they may lay up warships in the harbours of Port Said and Suez to a number not exceeding two of any nation.

Article 9. The representatives in Egypt of the powers who signed the treaty shall be charged with seeing to its a result of this, the neutralization of the Scandinavian kingdoms.

In connection with the neutralization of the Sound has arisen the still newer question of the non-German region north of the North Sea Canal, now in course of construction, between the mouth of the Elbe and the naval port of Kiel.

By constituting Elsass-Lothringen into an independent neutral State, a division would be made between France and Germany, and

fulfilment. In all cases where free passage through the canal may be menaced, they shall meet upon the summons of the senior member to investigate the facts. They shall acquaint the Khedive's Government with the danger anticipated, that it may take the measures needful to secure the safety and unimpeded use of the canal. They shall meet regularly once a year to ascertain that the treaty is properly observed. They shall most especially require the deposition of all works and dispersion of all collections of troops which on any part of the area of the canal might either design or cause a menace to the free passage or to the security thereof.

Article 10 treats of the obligations of the Egyptian Government and runs thus :—

The Egyptian Government shall, so far as its power by firman goes, take the measures necessary for enforcing the treaty. In case the Egyptian Government has not adequate means it shall apply to the Sublime Porte, which will then these great powers would be separated by a huge wall of neutral States which would also narrow in an essential degree the European battle-field.

The same result is hoped for from a confederacy of neutral States on the Balkan, with respect to the relations between Russia and Austria, as well as with respect to the whole of Europe.

The Sound is one of the most important arteries of the world's commerce. About one hundred vessels of all nations pass daily through this strait, but only about ten (on the average, however, certainly larger ships) pass through the Suez Canal, which in the interests of the world's trade has become neutral.

It can be nothing but a gain to Europe that the entrances both into the Baltic and the Black Sea should be rendered inviolate.

consult with the other signatories of the London treaty of March 17, and with them make provision in response to that application.

Article 14 sets forth : Beyond the duties expressed and stipulated for in the paragraphs of this treaty, the sovereign rights of his Imperial Majesty the Sultan are in no way curtailed, nor are the privileges and rights of his Highness the Khedive as defined by the firman.

In an address upon the importance of the Sound to the North, given to the National Economic Society, Mr. Bajer pointed out that so long as the Sound and its coasts were not rendered inviolate, military devastations will be carried on in and around the strait by belligerent powers; also that the facts that the Sound is not Danish only, but Swedish also, and that Sweden has a common foreign policy with Norway, make it probable that it may the sooner be understood to be for the European interest that all three northern kingdoms should be simultaneously neutralized, and not one of them only.[1]

In consequence of Mr. Bajer's indefatigable zeal for the united co-operation of the northern kingdoms in the cause of peace, this idea has gained many influential adherents in foreign countries also; and on his proposition, two international congresses, Geneva, Sept. 16th, 1883, and Berne, Aug. 6th, 1884, unanimously accepted the following resolution, which in its general meaning was adopted by the First

---

[1] Nationaloekonomisk Tidsskrift, xxii. pp. 139-155. See also *Politiken*, 1890, March 31. Article " Oeresunds Fred," signed, Defensor Patriæ.

Northern peace Meeting at Gotenberg, Aug. 19th, 1885 :—

Considering that,—

1. The geographical position of the three northern States, is such, that they might, with a larger military and commercial naval power than they now possess, hold the keys of the Baltic :

2. Whilst the very weakness of these States probably removes all danger of their using the advantages of this position against Europe, the same weakness may one day expose them, either by force or fraud, to be plundered by their powerful neighbours :

3. The inviolability of the three northern States, and their independence of every foreign influence, is in the true interest of all Europe, and their neutralization would tend to the general order.

4. Their independence, which is indeed a common right of all nations, can only be secured to the northern nations by their neutralization.

5. This neutralization ought to have for its object and legal effect :

   Firstly, To place beyond all danger of war all those portions of land and sea which belong to Sweden, Denmark and Norway.

   Secondly, To secure at all times, even during war, to all merchant and war-ships, whatever flag they carry, whether that of a belligerent or not, full liberty to run into the Baltic from the North Sea, or *vice versâ*, whether sailing singly or in fleets.

On these accounts the meeting declares,—

That Denmark, Sweden and Norway ought to be neutralized, and that this neutralization ought to include :—

1. With respect to the mainland and islands of Norway, Sweden and Denmark, that all parts of this territory shall be at all times entirely neutral.

2. With respect to the Sound and the Little Belt, that in time of war, ships belonging to any belligerent power shall be forbidden to show themselves in these seas ; which, on the other hand, shall be always open for merchant craft, even those belonging to belligerent powers, as well as for war-ships belonging to neutrals.

3. With respect to the Great Belt, that this strait shall always be open for merchant and war-ships of every flag, including belligerents, whether singly or in fleets ; but that these ships shall be entirely forbidden to undertake any inimical action on the coasts of the above-named strait, or in its seas, within a distance exceeding the maximum range of its artillery before sailing in or sailing out, or indeed any attack, seizure, privateering, blockade, embargo, etc., or any other warlike action whatever.

The meeting expressed its desire to see an international congress arrange and conclude a treaty which should be open for all European nations to enter into and sign, which should establish on the above-named basis, under the guarantee of the signatory powers, the neutrality of the northern States, together with the creation of a really solid tribunal of arbitration, which, as the highest court of appeal, should solve all difficulties that might arise with respect to the said treaty.

That the neutralization of the Suez Canal, so long looked upon as a pious wish, may in the near future lead to the inviolability of

Egypt, will doubtless be suggested. When this is accomplished, the good understanding between France and England will be further strengthened, and a foundation thereby laid for an extended co-operation in the service of the peace of the world, in the young Congo State, with its twenty millions of inhabitants and a territory equal to half Europe; a realm founded without costing a drop of blood, from its first commencement sanctioned and declared a neutral community by the European powers unanimously, which will some day be looked upon as one of the fairest pages in the history of the human race.

G

FURTHER DEVELOPMENTS.

In other ways the European powers have shown that, with a little willingness to do so, they can work together in the interests of peace.

We have an illustrative instance of this in the DANUBE COMMISSION, which, since 1856, has watched over the traffic in the Delta of the Danube, neutralized by the Treaty of Paris.

This commission, which is composed of members from all the great powers and Turkey and Roumania, and was originally appointed only for a short time, has, in consideration of its great value as an international institution, been renewed from year to year, and has had its power gradually extended. The commission possesses its own flag, its customs and pilotage, its police, its little fleet, and so on. It has for thirty years exercised an almost unlimited power over the mouths of the Danube, has made laws, raised a loan, carried out works, and in many other respects given evidence of the possibility of united co-operation amongst the powers under many changing and intricate international relations.

In the so-called EUROPEAN CONCERT is seen a commencement of an extended co-operation in a similar direction. The war between Servia and Bulgaria was confined within certain limits by the united will of the powers, and Greece was obliged to subdue her fierce military ardour.

Again, so far as concerns such coalitions as it is evident are not formed for the whole of Europe, but are said to aim at securing peace by accumulating forces, it could hardly be expected, from their very nature, that they would fulfil the alleged design in themselves. But, on the other side, it would be short-sighted to overlook their importance as a link in the gradually progressive development of the interests of various nations in the common concerns of Europe. One token in this direction is the proposal which was brought forward in the beginning of 1888 by a number of deputies in the Austrian Parliament, urging the Government, after procuring the consent of the Hungarian Government, to initiate negotiations with Germany for the purpose of getting

a GERMANO-AUSTRIAN ALLIANCE adopted by the
Parliaments of both realms, and constitu-
tionally incorporated in the fundamental law of
both States. This proposal may have hardly
any practical result, but it is worth notice as
one of the small rays of light which from time
to time point the way to a common goal.

Thither point too, though indeed from afar,
those propositions for DISARMAMENT which now
and then crop up, but which, quite naturally,
fade away as quickly as they come, so long as
the principle of arbitration does not prevail in
Europe.

"Europe's only salvation is a general disarmament," cries the illustrious Frenchman
Jules Simon, and yet louder the Italian ex-
minister, Bonghi. The latter a distinguished
Conservative statesman, utters these powerful
words in the *International Review* (Rome).

"The ideas of peace, which I have just expressed and
which are also entertained by the masses, sound almost
like a jest in the menaces of war which we hear around us.
And they are ridiculous if the policy which the Government
follows is considered serious. The great thing is to be able
to guess how long the ludicrous shall be regarded as
serious, and the serious as ludicrous; and how long a proceeding so devoid of sound reason as that of the great

European powers will be counted as sense. I, for my part, am persuaded that such a confusion as to the meaning of the words cannot endure continually, and that the present condition of things, whether people will or not, must soon cease. But we ought not to wait until the change is brought about by violence, nor indeed till it comes by violence from—below. Dynasties must give heed to this, and must hold me responsible for saying it—I, who am a royalist by conviction."

In the English House of Commons, Mr. A. Illingworth, May 30th, 1889, questioned the First Lord of the Treasury, Mr. W. H. Smith, "Whether the Government had recently made a proposal to the continental Governments that they should agree upon a considerable and early reduction of armaments? and with what result? And if not, whether Her Majesty's Government would without delay initiate such negotiations, having for their object to lessen the military burdens and the dangers which menace the peace of Europe."

In his answer the First Lord of the Treasury [1] said: "If any favourable opportunity manifested itself, the Government would have pleasure in using its influence in

[1] As an adherent of the Conservative party, he has always held to a strong armed force, and hardly ever supported peace efforts.

the direction indicated by the honourable
member.   But the questioner should bear in
mind, that an interference in a question of this
sort often does more harm than good to the
object he wishes to attain.   I can assure him
that the Government is as deeply impressed
with this question as himself, and it has often
expressed its view in the House, that the present armed condition of Europe is a great
misfortune and a danger to the peace of the
world."

In the German Parliament, also, similar
utterances may be heard ; in the latest instance
from one of the Centre, Reichensperger, who
in the military debate, June 28th, 1890, expressed the wish that they could set in motion
a general disarmament.   The speaker had
certainly spoken in favour of the Government
bill for adding 18,000 men to the peace footing
of the army.   But he wished alongside of that
to say, that as the decision of the Emperor in
summoning a conference of working men from
all parts of Europe had been greeted with applause, so would the civilized world, with still
greater applause greet the tidings that William
II. had advocated a general disarmament.

Many entertain the belief that the first condition of such a disarmament must be to absolve the rulers themselves from the dangerous power they possess in being able at their discretion to declare war, conclude peace, and make alliances one with another for warlike aims.

In our country many propositions have been brought forward for limiting this power especially with regard to the concluding of treaties without so much as consulting the whole Swedish Cabinet.

As is well known, even in the time of Gustavus Adolphus, the royal power did not extend beyond the king having to consult the Riksdag, and to obtain its consent, whether he were engaging in a war or entering into an alliance with foreign powers. The absolute monarchs seized upon greater power, and the law-makers of 1809 simply ratified this dangerous extension of it.

Now we are unceasingly told, when the subject of defence is on, about sacrifices. They declare to us that no sacrifice should be esteemed too great. The State has the right of enlisting soldiers by compulsion, fathers, husbands and sons, for the defence of the country ;

and not only when it is really a question of defence, but when it is a matter of preparation for defence, that is drill, even if this extend to years of barrack life in time of peace.

These are the sacrifices demanded from the people.

There are those who think, would it not be much better if the people, on their side, demanded a little security that the country should not be far too thoughtlessly plunged into war —war which can no longer be carried on by paid volunteers, but with members of families conscripted by force, by means of compulsory service?

Such security could be effected by changing the formulas of government §§ 12 and 13, and the constitutional law § 26, partly so that the conclusion of treaties should require the confirmation of a united meeting of the Swedo-Norse cabinet councils, and partly also, that certain treaties, namely such as include a greater political intricacy, should be subjected to the confirmation of the Riksdag and the Storting, as has been the case with certain treaties of commerce—bagatelles in comparison with the entanglement of the kingdoms in war.

It is simply an assertion, refuted by experience, that the king cannot make use of the law here treated of.

During the Crimean war, according to a treaty, we should have been entangled in the war, had not the Peace of Paris intervened. So also during the last Dano-German war, when interference on our part, as the result of a treaty, would have taken place, had not the death of King Frederic VII. occurred.

The same thing would have happened during the last Franco-German war, if the battle of Wörth had not thrown out the reckoning, according to a treaty which entailed our interference. Into all these treaties the king could enter without giving the whole Cabinet the opportunity of expressing its opinion.

The danger of such a power begins to be increasingly felt, especially in England. In 1886, Henry Richard raised in the House of Commons the question of abolishing the right of the sovereign to declare war without the consent of Parliament. The proposition was certainly rejected, but with the large minority of 109 against 115 votes. That the proposition could gather round it such a minority

may certainly be regarded as a remarkable
sign of the times. In 1889, W. R. Cremer
made a similar motion in the House. He proposed that a " parliamentary committee should
be chosen to examine and arrange foreign
matters, which were then to be laid before
Parliament." This proposal fell through ; but
progress was made, and Mr. Cremer still awaits.
a suitable occasion for renewing it.

A characteristic expedient is pointed out by
the well-known Belgian professor of political
economy, de Molinari, in an article published
in the *Times*.

He shows, in the first place, how solidarity
among the civilized States of the world has
lately increased in a marvellous degree, for not
long ago the foreign trade of a civilized nation
and the capital invested in other States was of
very small importance. Each country produced nearly all the requisites for its own
consumption, and employed its capital in its
own undertakings. In 1613, the whole of
England's imports and exports amounted to
only five million pounds sterling. A hundred
years later, indeed, the united foreign trade
of the whole of Europe did not amount to

so much as the present foreign trade of little
Belgium. Still more unimportant were the
foreign loans. Holland was the only country
whose capitalists lent to foreign Governments,
and persons were hardly to be found who ven-
tured to put their money into industrial undertakings in foreign lands, or even beyond the
provinces in which they dwelt. Consequently
at that time a neutral State suffered little or no
injury when two States were at war. A quarrel
between France and Spain or Germany then
did no more harm to English interests than a
war between China and Japan would do now.

At present it is quite otherwise. Trade and
capital have in our day become international.
While the foreign traffic of the civilized world
two hundred years ago did not exceed one hundred millions sterling, it runs up now to about
five thousand millions ; and foreign loans have
augmented in the same degree. In every
country there is a constantly increasing portion
of the population dependent for its subsistence
upon relations with other peoples, either for
the manufacture or exportation of goods, or
for the importation of foreign necessaries. In
France a tenth part of the population is depen-

dent in this way upon foreign countries, a third
in Belgium, and in England probably not far
from a third.

So long as there is peace, this increasing
community of interests is a source of well-
being, and advances civilization; but if a war
breaks out, that which was a blessing is turned
into a common ill. For, not to mention the
burden which preparations for defence impose
upon the neutral nations, they suffer from the
crisis which war causes in the money market,
and from the cessation or curtailing of their
trade with the belligerent powers.

From these facts, de Molinari deduces a
principle of justice—NEUTRAL STATES HAVE
THE RIGHT TO FORBID A WAR, as it greatly
injures their own lawful interests.

If two duellists fight out their quarrel in a
solitary place, where nobody can be injured by
their balls or swords, they may be allowed
without any great harm to exercise their right
of killing. But if they set to work to shoot
one another in a crowded street, no one can
blame the police if they interfere, since their
action exposes peacable passers-by to danger.
It is the same with war between States. Neu-

tral States would have small interest in hinder-
ing war, if war did not do them any particular
harm; and under those circumstances their right
to interfere might be disputed. But when, as
is now the case, war cannot be carried on without menacing a great and constantly increasing
portion of the interests of neutrals, yes, even
their existence, their right to come in and
maintain order is indisputable.

The worst is that, after all, the belligerent
nation itself never decides its own fate. That
is settled by a few politicians and military men,
who have quite other interests than those of
business. It is often done by a single man;
and it may be said without exaggeration, that
the world's peace depends upon the pleasure
of three or four men, sovereigns or ministers,
who can any day, at their discretion, let slip all
the horrors of war. They can thereby bring
measureless misery and ills upon the whole
civilized world's peaceable industries, not except-
ing even those of neutral nations, with whom
they have nothing to do. The most absolute
despots of the rude old times had no such power.

Self-interests of purely political nature give
the neutral States, especially the smaller ones,

the right to do what they can to prevent war between other powers; because it is an old experience that war among the great powers readily spreads itself to the little ones.

De Molinari states further that the neutral States may so much the more easily ward off all this evil, as they have not only the right, but also the power, if they would set themselves to do it.

Thereupon he unfolds his proposition :—

"With England at the head, and with Holland, Belgium, Switzerland and Denmark as members, there might be formed a confederation, 'THE NEUTRAL LEAGUE,' for the purpose of attacking any of the other powers who should begin a war, and of helping the attacked. The States named have a united strength of 460,000 men, and can place on a war footing 1,200,000. To these may be added the fleets of England, Holland and Denmark, which together form the strongest naval power in the world." [1]

[1] That he does not take in the Scandinavian peninsula, must be because he regards the position of the northern kingdoms as too remote from the continental quarrels to be sensibly disturbed by them; or because he has not a high opinion of the fitness of their military forces for attack, which is here alluded to.

Suppose that a complication takes place
between two great powers on the continent of
Europe—Germany, France, Austria, or Russia
—there can be no doubt that if the " League "
united its strength with the threatened power,
that power would become thereby so superior
to its opponent that victory would be certain.

For this reason a peaceable interference on
the part of the League before the war broke
out, would make the most warlike amongst the
powers consider.

But the fact that no State could stir up a
war without meeting a crushing superior force
would lead to a constant and lasting state of
peace, and disarmament.

De Molinari thinks his plan would be
advanced by forming an association in the
countries named, which should work for an
agreement between them in the above-named
direction.

The proposition will never of itself lead to
any practical result. But it is at least useful
in having pointed out the growing interest
which neutral powers have in maintaining
peace unmolested. This interest shows itself
already in general politics in the zealous pains

with which, on the outbreak of war, all powers not implicated unite to " localize" war, that is, to limit it to as few partisans, and to as small an area, as possible. The peace interests of neutral States become year by year more powerful factors in politics.

Here we must bear in mind that more States are continually passing over into the condition of unconsciously forming " a neutral league." They are approaching the goal which they have long been striving after by arms and by diplomacy. " They are," to quote Bismarck, " satisfied and do not strive for more." Such States are Germany and Italy, which have achieved their unity, and Hungary, which has gained its freedom.

Nevertheless all great causes of war are not thereby eradicated from Europe.

In the forenamed article by the Russian jurist, Kamarowski, light is thrown upon this circumstance with scientific clearness.

He says respecting Germany, that this country has essentially realized its national unity, and thereby reached a justifiable object; but at the same time has been guilty of two serious violations of the principles of international right.

" It carried on the war against France with an inflexible and altogether unnecessary severity, and it tore from that State Elsass-Lothringen."

The attempt is certainly made to justify this by the fact that both these provinces formerly belonged to Germany, and that it was an absolute necessity for Germany to acquire a military guarantee against a fresh attack on the part of France.

Kamarowski shows both these grounds to be untenable. If nations should continually look back to the past, and strive to renew the old conditions, they never could found a more durable or righteous state of things in the present.

What ought to be decisive is, that in these unhappy provinces the sympathy of the great part of the population is completely on the side of France.

The possession of Strasburg and Metz has not only failed to give Germany the anticipated security; it has, on the other hand, compelled the Germans to live since 1871 in perpetual unrest; to keep on foot an immense army, and to expend their last resources in building fortresses. Besides, this possession cripples Ger-

man activity in both internal and external
political questions. The situation of France
is equally unenviable ; constantly kept in suspense, and with the feeling of having been
unjustly treated, and longing for revenge. Is
it possible, with this deadly hatred between two
of Europe's most civilized states, to think of a
lasting peace?

And what can the Governments of these
nations do with respect to this evil, unless they
set themselves to eradicate it ?

Kamarowski proposes three different solu-
tions of the question of Elsass-Lothringen. A
European congress might arrange the destiny
of these provinces, by dividing them, for example, so that Elsass should remain united to
Germany, and Lothringen to France ; or by
forming them into two or more cantons united
to Switzerland ; or lastly, by letting them become an independent State with a self-chosen
mode of government, but with the *sine quâ non*
that they shall be neutralized, and placed under
the guarantee of combined Europe.

It would be almost immaterial to Europe
which of these three expedients were chosen ;
therefore the choice might be left to the inhab-

itants of Elsass-Lothringen themselves; and the opportunity might be given them of expressing themselves by a plebiscite, uncontrolled by any influence from either the French or German side.

This naturally affects Danish South Jutland in an equal degree, which Germany wrenched from Denmark by a gross breach of international law. That the writer does not adduce this instance may be simply because he does not regard it as involving any danger of war.

Kamarowski finds this to be much more pronounced with regard to the EASTERN QUESTION.

This is more threatening than that of Elsass-Lothringen. Ever since the close of the last century the Turkish Empire has, on account of its internal condition, been doomed to fall to pieces, and its final dissolution is only a question of time. It is difficult to say what is to be done with the remains.

The only reasonable and righteous settlement is to allow the Christian peoples who were in the past subjected by the Turks, and who compose the great majority of the population in European Turkey, to form independent

States. Manifold causes have hitherto prevented the organization of the political life of
these nations, shorn of political maturity in
consequence of protracted thraldom, mutual
jealousy, and influences of the great powers,
who under all manner of excuses have played
their own game at the cost of these people,
pretending to protect them, while they sought
to make them into their subjects. Russia
has doubtless, even if unintentionally, in the
greatest degree helped to set these nations
free, and to produce the present position by
which Servia and Roumania have been changed,
from being subject to Turkey, into independent
States; and Bulgaria, instead of being a Turkish
province, has now a less subject position as
regards Turkey. "It is," says the writer, "not
altogether without reason that the Russians
accuse their Southern Sclav brethren of in-
gratitude"; but he admits that Russia ought
partly to blame herself. She has, for instance,
at times shown a decided inclination to force
her forms of thought and policy upon them,
and to get the whole of their inner national life
placed under her authority. This action of Russia is blameworthy, both because it violates the

independence which belongs of right to every
State, and because it is foolishly opposed to Russia's own well-known interests. By such a policy
she can only betray her Sclav mission, create
more than one new Poland for herself, and artifi-
cially shift her political power from north to
south, thereby weakening her national strength.

Kamarowski further describes the selfish
schemes of England and Austria in the Balkan
peninsula.

These plans are even more distasteful to
the Christian population than Russia's, because
it stands in the closest relation to that country
both as to race and a common religion. England and Austria seek to entice this people
by the prospect of freer institutions and greater
economic well-being; but they can only drag
them into their net at the cost of their national
and moral independence. And the jealousy
between these powers, Russia on the one hand
and Austria and England on the other, each
wanting to get the advantage, or to possess
itself of the remains of the dying realm, is a
standing menace to the peace of Europe. This
danger would disappear if people could be satisfied to let these nations belong to themselves.

Now that Austria has carried out the injunction laid upon her by the Berlin Congress—for the present to undertake the management and administration of Bosnia and Herzegovina— she ought to withdraw from these provinces, whose population should be allowed to decide their own fate by universal suffrage, whether this would result in the union of Bosnia with Servia, and of Herzegovina with Montenegro, or whether the situation should be arranged in some other way. All that Austria has any ground for requiring is, the free navigation of the Danube and the straits (Bosphorus and Dardanelles), and therewith her true interests in this region would be abundantly satisfied.

The Christian States which, alongside of Turkey, have spread over the Balkan peninsula, are Greece, Roumania, Servia, Montenegro and Bulgaria. The last named still stands in subjection to Turkey, but has the same right to full independence as the neighbour States. It is evidently their vocation to divide amongst themselves the remains of Turkey in Europe, for their population in an overwhelming proportion consists of Southern Sclavs and Greeks. But unhappily they seem to have

little conception of this their task, because they
live in a constant state of jealousy and bicker-
ing. These States are all only just in the
embryo. They have not yet by a long way
attained their natural boundaries. A large
number of Greeks and Bulgarians are still
under the direct government of Turkey. It
would be labour lost to attempt to guess how
many small States will form themselves out of
the ruins of Turkey, or what political form they
will take. The author remarks that it would
be best for them to arrange themselves into
one or more confederations with self-govern-
ment for each single State composing this alliance.

Europe, in harmony with international
justice, should see to it : (1) that the peoples of
the Balkan peninsula should not become the
prey of any foreign power; (2) that they should
not be allowed to trespass upon each other's
domains; (3) that their development should
as far as possible proceed in a peaceful and
law-abiding way; (4) that they should divide
the inheritance of Turkey in a thoroughly just
manner, so that the political boundaries should
be marked out in harmony with the wishes

and interests of the inhabitants ; (5) that they themselves do not invade the domains of other States, and that they recognise all the maxims of international justice.

A European congress, co-operating in such an arrangement of the conditions of the Balkan peninsula, would contribute in no small degree to remove the causes of war in Europe, and would do effective work in the cause of freedom and civilization. Greece would acquire all the islands of the Archipelago, together with Candia and Cyprus. Macedonia would, according to the conditions of its nationalities, be divided between Greece and Bulgaria. The natural boundary of the latter would be the Danube on the one side and the Archipelago on the other. Constantinople would remain the capital of a Bulgarian kingdom, or of a Southern Sclav federation ; or again, a free city with a small independent territory.[1] The

---

[1] According to the proposal of an old diplomatist, the Sultan should be given a similar position in Constantinople to that of the Pope, now, in Rome. Thereby the Sultan would become innocuous to Europe, but continue to be the "Ruler of the Faithful" to Asia. ("La question d'Orient devant l'Europe democratique." Paris : E. Dentu, *libraire*, 1886).

fortifications on both sides the Bosphorus and
Dardanelles should be destroyed, and both
these straits be thrown open to the navigation
of all nations.

After being obliterated from the list of
European nations, Turkey would peacefully
continue its existence in Asia.

But not even so are all the causes of war
removed from our continent. Many are to be
found in the RELATIONS BETWEEN RUSSIA AND
ENGLAND ; especially two, says Kamarowski.

One is the opposition between the dissimilar
forms of government in these countries. England is the advocate of liberal social institutions
all over the continent, but Russia poses as the
mainstay of unlimited sovereign power and of
conservative principles. Yet doubtless Russia
will sooner or later, with a firmness and con-
sistency hitherto lacking, strike into the path of
political reform, and then this contrast will be
assimilated.

The other consists in the opposing interests
of the two powers upon the Eastern Question.
But if this question is solved as the author proposes, by the whole Balkan peninsula being
permitted to form itself into independent States

under the guarantee of united Europe, this cause of strife would also be removed. Russia need no longer threaten India. Russia's true well-being can never consist in spreading herself over the deserts and wastes of Asia, or in the endless compulsory subjection of hostile races under her. She will doubtless in time perceive this.

Historical facts have already marked out the domain of both realms and the boundaries of their influence. The greater part of Southern Asia is more or less subjected to England. The whole of Northern and Central Asia belongs to Russia. Russia and England have a common mission in Asia—to promote the Christian civilization of the world; and in this direction each has her special call.

Also in the relations between RUSSIA AND GERMANY are found indeed inflammable materials; but with wise action on both sides they may be got rid of.

Russia has, more than any other power, promoted the unity and powerful position of Germany. Except during the strife between the Empress Elizabeth and Frederic II., constant friendly relations have obtained between Russia and Prussia; so, under Frederick II. and Catherine II., and during Prussia's struggle against Napoleon I.; while the friendship between Alexander II. and William I. made possible the wars of 1866 and 1870-71. The House of Hohenzollern, which has never been any friend of popular freedom, felt drawn to Russia upon the ground of its devotion to conservative modes of thought and its absolutism.

But since Prussia has realized her goal—that of being the leading power in Germany—the relations with Russia have become more and more strained.

One of the chief causes has been the disputes caused by economic questions, and that of the customs in particular.

In addition to this is the general misunderstanding fomented by the press. The political press, says Kamarowski, ought to serve the cause of peace to-day more than ever. Unhappily it by no means does. With few exceptions it helps to fan and feed national hatred, and to stir up enmity between the European States. Most of the principal organs have a narrower horizon than this. Some of these papers and periodicals are worked only as business undertakings, to make the greatest possible profit to the shareholders ; the best of them defend with gross one-sidedness the interests of their own country; seldom do they disclose any insight into great, purely humanitarian interests. The political press is, therefore, for the most part a constant source of reciprocal suspicion and hatred, which hinders the States of Europe from entering into the condition of peace they all inwardly so long for. Dip at random into a heap of most of the great papers, and you will find the strangest ideas respecting international justice ; rank self-assertion in judgment, and purely barbarous sentiments respecting subjugating and destroying so-called hereditary enemies.

Lastly, there is a cause of tension between Russia and Germany in their opposing attitude with regard to the Sclav question ; and if a satisfactory solution is not found for this question in a peaceable way, a crowd of complications will arise, into which Russia will inevitably be drawn.

We have first the Polish question. In our day Russia is entering, through the power of circumstances, more and more into her historic vocation of giving freedom and unity to the Sclavs. But this undertaking stands in direct opposition to the policy which was expressed in the partition of Poland.

Russia's future *rôle* may be to favour a confederation of all the Sclav peoples. Her true mission cannot be to subdue or trample down any Sclav nationality, but much rather to emancipate them all. Emancipate from what? From the yoke of Turkey and of Germany. So far as the former is concerned, a great part of the work has been already carried out. With regard to the Germans, Russia cannot think of the restoration of the disputed and long obliterated boundaries of the Sclav races, which were lost in the struggle with the Germans; but she may assist the organization of the bodies politic of the Sclav races, and co-operate in revivifying those branches of the nation which are not altogether dead.

The author desires, therefore, that Poland should be restored by Russia's own act. Yet Poland must not demand her boundaries as they were before 1772 (that is, the possession of Lithuania). Once admitted into a

Sclav confederation, she would cease to be a menace to any one, but would serve as a bulwark between Russia and Germany.

The solution of the Sclav question might, according to the author's idea, bring with it the dismemberment of the Austrian Empire. The German part would go to Germany, and Trieste and South Tyrol fall to Italy. Austria's Sclav provinces would be acknowledged as independent, and either unite themselves with the Sclav federation on the Balkan peninsula, or form a separate State. The situation in Bohemia would be the most difficult to arrange, since in part it is a German-speaking country; but as a Sclav land, it ought under no circumstances to be entirely given over to the Germans. Hungary also would obtain its independence, but must, on its own part, recognise the freedom of Croatia. The inhabitants of the various portions of the Austrian Empire would themselves have to decide their fate, and in the interests of all, a European congress should be summoned, to maintain the general peace, and to prevent one nationality from subjecting or swallowing up another.

But while Professor Kamarowski here and

elsewhere in his treatise speaks of congresses, he does not mean thereby the meetings of diplomatists to which that name now applies.

Congresses ought, he says, to be actual international organs, whose object is not to serve the fluctuating and conflicting interests of policy, but the strict principles of justice. They must be permanent institutions, and being so, help on international reforms, such as a gradual disarmament and a codification of international law; that is, a correct digest of the various regulations and principles of international law, forming a common law for all civilized nations.

In the last named direction there is in the field already THE ASSOCIATION FOR THE REFORM AND CODIFICATION OF INTERNATIONAL LAW, founded at Brussels, Oct. 10th, 1873, and in an important degree consisting of the most eminent jurists of the nations. This association, which meets annually for the discussion of international law in various parts of Europe, deals also with the scholarly inquiry into the continually growing material, springing from the many international congresses, which so often now, with various objects, meet first in one part

then in another of the civilized world. As
examples of some of the most recent of these
may be named :   The post and telegraph conferences ; the conference on maritime law in
Washington, representing twenty-one separate
States, with the purpose of working out a
universal system of signals for preventing
collisions ; the African conference at Brussels,
with representatives of most of the European
powers for considering the best way of civilizing Africa, getting rid of the slave trade, and
limiting the exportation of alcohol ; [1] the railway meeting at Lugano, for introducing a
uniform time table and scale of freight, on all
railways of the European continent ; the Madrid
conference, for international protection of
industrial property, and above all the Labour
Congress held at Berlin by William II.'s invitation.

[1] In the United States Congress, Mr. Blaine has introduced a bill for calling an international conference in
Washington, in 1891, for making an alliance, whose object
is the suppression of slavery and the prohibition of alcohol
in uncivilized countries.   The conference is further to dis-
cuss the creation of a tribunal of Arbitration, for the
solution of international questions, and a general
disarmament.

Whilst in this way the nations' own desire and the needs of the case grow and branch into great common interests, the friends of peace unceasingly set before themselves this distinct goal, "Right before might."

To paint the historic background of the activity of the friends of peace would be almost synonymous with bringing forward all that is uniting, important and lasting in the history of the nations. It would be a "saga" on the welfare of the human race through all time. Such a task I do not undertake. I give only a short indication of what, in our own time, organized peace-work is.

Its activity was almost a result of the wars of Napoleon, which were terminated by the Peace of Paris, November, 1815. These wars had deeply stirred the minds of many, both in the old and new world, and directed their thoughts to the apathy of the Christian Churches in not proclaiming, with unmistakable emphasis, that war is irreconcilable with the teaching of Christ.

This view was represented in America by Dr. W. ELLERY CHANNING, and Dr. NOAH WORCESTER, who as early as 1814 stirred up

I

the friends of peace to organize themselves into united work.

A Peace Society was formed in New York in August, 1815; and in November of the same year the Ohio Peace Society. The Massachusetts Peace Association (Boston) started in January, 1816, and a similar society was begun in Rhode and Maine in 1817. These, with that of South Carolina, united in 1828, and formed the AMERICAN PEACE SOCIETY, an association which is still in active operation. Also in Philadelphia an association was formed, which was succeeded in 1868 by the UNIVERSAL PEACE UNION.

In 1814 a zealous philanthropist, Mr. William Allen, a member of the Society of Friends, invited a number of persons to his house in *London* to form a peace association. They did not at once agree upon the best method, and the proposal was deferred for a time. But after the conclusion of peace was signed in 1816, Mr. Allen, with the assistance of his friend Mr. Joseph Tregelles Price, also a member of the Society of Friends, called his friends together again, and succeeded in bringing into existence the English peace association, under the name of the PEACE SOCIETY.

The source from which the association sprang is to be found in the Society of Friends (Quakers), that sect which has always been a faithful proclaimer of the peace principles of Christianity. But the founders were not all of this society. Some were members of the Church of England and of other religious persuasions.

As the foundation of its effort, the association advanced the great principle that war is contrary to the spirit of Christianity and to the true interests of mankind. It has always been open to persons of all persuasions. One of its first stipulations was, that " the society shall consist of all ranks of society who will unite in forwarding peace on earth and good-will amongst men." The association has always been international. From its commencement it proclaimed its desire to bring other nations as far as possible within the reach of its operations. Some of the first acts of the founders were to translate its most important writings into French, German, Spanish and Italian.

Immediately after, in 1816, Mr. J. T. Price, the most zealous amongst the founders, undertook a journey to *France* to gain adhesion and

co-operation amongst Christians and philan-
thropists in that country. Many hindrances
lay in the way of forming an association in
that country which should have peace only for
its object. These difficulties were overcome
by founding a Society of Christian Morals (*La*
Société de morale Chrétienne), whose aim was to
bring the teaching of Christianity to bear upon
the social question. This society continued for
more than a quarter of a century and numbered
amongst its members many illustrious French-
men. Its first president was the Duke of
Rochefoucauld-Liancourt; its vice-president
was the Marquis of the same name, the son
of the above. Amongst the members were
Benjamin Constant, the Duke of Broglie, de
Lamartine, Guizot, Carnot, and Duchatel.
The promotion of peace was one of the objects
of the Society.

A branch of it was formed in *Geneva*, under
the leadership of Count Sellon, and the English parent society stood in close and lively
connection with both these associations. It
had for many years in its service an active man,
Stephen Rigaud, who travelled through France,
Belgium, Germany and Holland, held meetings,

distributed tracts, and formed committees and associations in furtherance of peace.

Between the years 1848 and 1851 a still greater aggressive peace movement was set on foot upon the European continent, by means of congresses held at Brussels, Paris and Frankfort, and by the attendance of many hundred delegates from all the countries of Europe.

This effort for peace was entered upon by the Secretary, Mr. Henry Richard. At least twenty times he visited the Continent, speaking for peace and arbitration in many, if not most, of the largest cities—Paris, Berlin, Vienna, Pesth, Dresden, Leipsic, Munich, Frankfort, Brussels, Antwerp, Bremen, Cologne, the Hague, Amsterdam, Genoa, Rome, Florence, Venice, Milan, Turin, etc.

These efforts bore good fruit. The friends of peace began to stir. Peace societies were formed, devoted attachments were made, and personal intercourse created between the adherents of peace principles in various lands.

This was especially the case in France, where *la Ligue Internationale de la Paix* was founded by M. Frédéric Passy. In 1872 the name of the league was changed to the

Société Française des Amis de la Paix. This name it retained until its amalgamation with the *Comité de Paris de la Fédération Internationale de l'Arbitrage et de la Paix*, founded by Mr. Hodgson Pratt in 1883. The new society, formed of the union of the two, bears the name of the *Société Française de l'Arbitrage entre Nations.*

The *Ligue Internationale de la Paix et de la Liberté* was founded at Geneva by M. Charles Lemonnier as far back as 1867. Under the powerful leadership of this aged captain of peace the league has, by its activity in promoting the idea of the "United States of Europe," constantly sought to work in a practical way for its object,—peace and freedom.

The same year, too, were founded the *Ligue du Désarmement* and the *Union de la Paix*, at Havre.

But the most remarkable occurrence in this domain was the spontaneous interchange of addresses and greetings between workmen in France and Germany, which led to the formation, in Biebrich on the Rhine, of an ASSOCIATION OF GERMAN AND FRENCH WORKING-MEN.

As a result of a visit from Mr. Richard three years later, there was founded at the Hague, Sept. 8th, 1870, " THE DUTCH PEACE SOCIETY," by Mr. Van Eck and others. Later in the same year ten similar associations sprang up in the Hague, Amsterdam, Zwolle, Groningen and other places. One of these, the " Women's Peace Society," in Amsterdam, under the leadership of Miss Bergendahl, deserves to be named, on account of its advanced character. In 1871 this union took the name of the " *Peace Society's National Union for Holland,*" and in 1878 of the " Peace League of the Netherlands." Its present name is the " *Universal Peace Association for the Netherlands*" (*Algemeen Nederlandsch Vredesbond*). For seventeen years Mr. Geo. Belinfante as the indefatigable secretary of this Union. He died in 1888, and was succeeded by M. C. Bake, of the Hague.

In 1871 the BELGIAN ASSOCIATION was formed at Brussels, and at the same time a local association at Verviers. Later on, April 15th, 1889, was founded the Belgian branch of the International Arbitration and Peace Association (*Fédération Internationale de l Arbitrage*

et de la Paix, section Belge), under the leadership of M. E. de Laveleye.

The ENGLISH PARENT SOCIETY has, in the
course of three-quarters of a century, employed
every means that can serve to advance a public
cause. By lectures and public meetings ; by
the distribution of literature and a diligent use
of the press ; by appeals to the peoples ; petitions to the Governments ; resolutions in parliament ; by adapting themselves to Sunday
and other schools, by influencing the religious
community, the clergy and teachers ; by combinations and interviews with peace friends in
all lands—by all practicable means it has
sought to work towards its goal.

First and foremost, it has advocated arbitration as a substitute for war, laboured for the final
establishment of an International Law, and a
Tribunal for the nations, and for a gradual reduction of standing armies ; at the same time
it has never ceased to raise its voice against the
wars in which England and other nations have
engaged. At a Universal International Peace
Congress, held in London under the auspices of
the society in 1843, it was resolved to send an
address "to the Governments of the civilized

world," whereby they should be earnestly con-jured to consider the principle of arbitration, and to recognise it. This address was sent to forty-five Governments. By a deputation to the powers at the Paris Congress in 1856, this society succeeded, as before said, in getting the principle of arbitration recognised, etc.

From the commencement, the English and American peace societies have worked side by side with brotherly concord. There are over forty peace societies in America. Besides these already named—viz., the *American Peace Society*, and the *Universal Peace Union*—the following are most important : *The Christian Arbitration and Peace Society*, Philadelphia ; *the National Arbitration League*, Washington; *the American Friends' Peace Society*, for Indiana and Ohio, founded December 1, 1873 ; and *the International Code Committee*, New York, of which David Dudley Field is president.

On the 25th of July, 1870, the English WORKMEN'S PEACE ASSOCIATION, now called the INTERNATIONAL ARBITRATION LEAGUE, was founded by members of the "Reform League," a great union of workmen in London. Two years later this Arbitration League, under Mr. W.

R. Cremer's powerful leadership, had well-appointed local associations all over the country, and nearly a hundred zealous leaders in various towns. Since then Mr. Cremer has become a Member of Parliament, and as such has had the opportunity of helping the peace cause in many ways ; for example, as a zealous participant in the deputation of twelve to the President of the United States, which has been mentioned more particularly in the beginning of this work.

In April, 1874, was formed the WOMEN's AUXILIARY OF THE PEACE SOCIETY. This continued to work in connection with the English parent society until 1882, when a division took place. Part of the members gathered themselves into an auxiliary, now called the LOCAL PEACE ASSOCIATION AUXILIARY OF THE PEACE SOCIETY, which has thirty-three sub-associations in England only. The other part formed the WOMEN'S PEACE AND ARBITRATION ASSOCIATION.[1]

At the same time great progress was made upon the Continent.

[1] Since amalgamated with the Women's Committee of the International Arbitration and Peace Association.

In Italy a LEAGUE OF PEACE AND BROTHER-
HOOD was founded as early as 1878, by Signor
E. T. Moneta.

A workmen's peace association was formed
at Paris in 1879, by M. Desmoulins and others,
under the name of the *Société des travailleurs
de la Paix.*

At the close of 1882, The DANISH PEACE
SOCIETY, or " Society for the Neutralization of
Denmark," was founded in Copenhagen, with
FREDRIK BAJER, M.P., as chairman, and twenty-
five local associations in Denmark.[1] There is
also at Copenhagen a " Women's Progress
Society," which, with Mrs. Bajer as president,
placed the cause of peace prominently upon
its programme.

At a meeting of members of the Riksdag, in
the spring of 1883, a SWEDISH PEACE SOCIETY
was formed, which has for its object to co-
operate with the *International Arbitration and
Peace Association* of Great Britain and Ireland,
in working for the preservation of peace among
nations, and the establishment of an International Tribunal of Arbitration, under the mutual
protection of the States, to which disputes that

[1] For the objects of this Association see Appendix.

may arise may be referred.   The first chairman
of the society was S. A. HEDLUND, who has long
laboured in Sweden for the spread of informa-
tion as to the efforts of the friends of peace.

The same year a NORWEGIAN PEACE SOCIETY
was formed, which, however, like the Swedish
sister association, has been apparently only
dead-alive of late.

This is the result, certainly in great degree,
of the slender interest taken by the cultivated
classes, who in general pose as either indifferent
or antagonistic to peace work ; indifferent, because, in ignorance of the subject, they look
upon organized peace effort as fanciful and
fruitless ; antagonistic, because they see in these
efforts a hindrance to getting the national defence strengthened by increased military forces.
As regards Norway, there are, however, signs
that a different view of things has lately begun
to make itself felt.[1]

In France the peace societies received
strength in 1884, through the foundation by M.
GODIN of the *Société de Paix et d'Arbitrage*

---

[1] "On August 8th, 1891, at a meeting at Seljord, a New
Norwegian Peace Association was formed, and a provisional
Committee appointed." TRANS.

International du Familistère de Guise (Aisne), Godin's activity has embraced not less than forty-two departments in France. Besides these may be named the *Société d'Aide Fraternelle et d'Etudes Sociales,* the *Société de Paix par l'Education* at Paris, the *Groupe des Amis de la paix à Clermont-Ferrand, La Fraternité Universelle* Grammond, Canton de St. Galmier (Loire), and the *Association des Jeunes Amis de la Paix,* Nîmes.

The INTERNATIONAL ARBITRATION AND PEACE ASSOCIATION for Great Britain and Ireland was founded in 1880.[1] This association, with which the Scandinavian society should co-operate the most closely, has a worthy chairman in Mr. HODGSON PRATT, a man whose devoted and untiring zeal has made him a distinguished leader of the peace movement, to which he has dedicated the whole business of his life.

His sphere of action has also included the Continent, and borne good fruit. Amongst others he succeeded in instituting peace societies at DARMSTADT, STUTTGART and FRANKFORT ; a committee of the association at BUDAPEST ; and in ROME, the *Associazione per l'*

---

[1] For programme of the Association see Appendix.

Arbitrato e la Pace tra le Nazione, with RUGGIERO BONGHI as president; and also in MILAN, the *Unione Lombarda per la Pace e l' Arbitrato Internazionale*.

In the course of the last three years, 1886–90, the idea of peace has made great progress in Italy. The movement has not been confined to any special class of society, or to any particular political or religious party, but has spread alike amongst all.

In the autumn of 1888 the central committee of the *Italian League of Peace and Liberty* sent out a leaflet, with a protest against any war with France. The central committee, which numbers amongst its members, senators, deputies, and many of Garibaldi's former companions in arms, declares : " The league requires all Italians, young and old, women and men, philosophers, tradesmen and working men, to unite all their energies in the great work of peace ; that there may be an end of armaments, which are a positive ruin to all nations."

In the course of 1889 several important peace congresses were held. In Milan, such a congress met for the first time, January 13th, representing 200 associations in France, Italy,

and Spain ; and for the second time, April 28th,
when fifty-four Italian societies were represented. Eight days after the first Milan meeting, a similar one took place in Naples, attended
by 3,000 persons, which expressed the united
views of five hundred associations.

Lastly, a congress was held in Rome, May
10-14, which represented thirty-nine peace
associations, the ex-minister Bonghi in the
chair. The meeting expressed the desire that
governments would find means to diminish the
war burdens by international agreements similar
to those by which economic and scientific
matters are already arranged, as well as questions dealing with general sanitary concerns.
A committee, consisting of six senators and
deputies, was afterwards chosen for further
work in the cause of peace.

A specially noteworthy feature in these
Italian peace congresses is the deep repugnance
to the Triple Alliance—which is regarded as a
standing menace of war,—and a strong craving
for good relations with France.

The way to this lies through increased
peaceful connection. This was especially
manifest in the meeting at Rome, which had

to prepare for the participation of Italians in the Peace Congress at Paris in the summer of 1889.

The Congresses of 1889 formed part of the great commemoration of the Revolution ; that meeting of international fraternity which, in the words of President Carnot in his opening speech, " shall hasten the time when the resources of the nations, and the labour of mankind, shall be dedicated only to the works of peace."

One of these gatherings, the Universal Peace Congress, June 23–27, which was composed of delegates from the peace societies of Europe and America, had, amongst other vocations, to express itself on certain general principles for carrying forward the idea of arbitration. It specially maintained and emphasized that the principle of arbitration ought to form a part of fundamental law in the constitution of every State.[1]   Before the meeting closed, it

---

[1] This principle is likely to be realized by the bill of the constitution of the Brazilian Republic, sanctioned by the executive of the new free State, which proclaims that the Government may not begin a war without having first appealed to arbitration.

was decided that the next Universal Congress should be held in London in 1890.

The other assembly, an INTERPARLIAMEN-TARY CONFERENCE (June 29–30), composed ex-clusively of legislators from many lands, was entitled to express itself more definitely on the adoption of actual measures ; notably, on the best means of bringing about arbitration treaties between certain States and groups of States.

With this Interparliamentary Conference, this international parliamentary meeting, we come to the beginning of a new and exalted organization, forming almost a powerful prelude to co-operation between England, America and France, such as I spoke of in the com-mencement of this book.

After the emissaries of the 270 members of the legislature had in the autumn of 1887 fulfilled their mission to America, and had started an active movement there which has since spread over the whole American con-tinent, English and French representatives of the people met in Paris, October 31st, 1888, and decided on behalf of many hundreds of their absent associates that a meeting of members of as many parliaments as possible should take place during the Universal Exposition in 1889.

This resolution was carried into effect. On June 20th about one hundred parliamentary representatives assembled in Paris from Belgium, Denmark, England, France, Hungary, Italy, Liberia, the United States and Spain. Nearly four hundred members of various parliaments had given their adhesion to the design of the meeting. Jules Simon opened the proceedings. Many important resolutions were passed, with a view to practically carrying into effect the principle of arbitration. After this it was arranged that a similar assembly should meet annually in one or other of the capital cities of the countries in sympathy; in 1890, in London; and lastly, a committee of forty was chosen, composed, according to resolution, of six members of every nationality, which should undertake the preparation of the next conference, send out the invitations, collect the necessary contributions, and in the interim do all in their power to remove the misunderstandings which might possibly arise, when it appealed, as it would be needful to do, to public opinion

Pursuant to the invitation of this committee, the second International Assembly of Members of Parliament met in London, July 22–23, 1890.

In consequence of the second Universal Peace Congress, the central gathering of the peace societies, being held only a short time previously (July 14–19), a large number of influential men attended this international meeting of legislators; but whilst amongst those who took part in the first named conference, the Universal Peace Congress, were a fair number of M.P.s of various countries, yet (with few exceptions) all those who took part in the interparliamentary meeting were members of one or other national legislative assembly.

The second Interparliamentary Conference, in London, 1890, had double the attendance of the first, in Paris,—members from Austria, Belgium, Denmark, England, France, Germany, Holland, Hungary, Italy, Norway, Spain and Sweden; besides which, more than a thousand representatives of the people, who were prevented attending, signified by letter their adhesion. Amongst these were Gladstone, Clemenceau, the Vice-president of the German Reichstag, Baumbach, the Italian Prime

Minister Crispi, Andrassy, and three French Ministers. Ninety-four Italian senators and deputies, and thirty-one members of the Spanish Cortes, in their respective addresses, expressed their sympathy with the work of the conference. The ex-Lord Chancellor, Lord Herschell, acted as chairman.

The most important resolution of the meeting was, that all civilized governments were urged to refer all disputes in which they might be involved to arbitration for solution.

Those present bound themselves to work to the best of their ability for the object, especially through the press and in the national assembly of their own lands, and thus gradually win public opinion over to the cause.

As a first step towards practically settling international disputes by arbitration, the conference urged that in all treaties affecting trade, literature, or other arrangements, a special arbitral clause should be inserted.

Amongst other resolutions it was voted, that a parliamentary committee should be created in each country for mutual consultation on international matters.

Lastly, a standing interparliamentary committee of thirty members was chosen, to serve as a connecting link in the interval between the conferences.

The third Interparliamentary Conference will meet in Rome in 1891.

In the fact that these conferences are composed of legislators chosen by the people lies their peculiar significance. They speak with power, because they are supported by millions of electors in various lands. The weight of their utterances naturally increases in the proportion in which the number of members grows. As yet this parliament of the peoples represents only a minority of the national assemblies; but the day may be coming when it will express the opinion of the majority, and that would be the triumph of right over might.

In the effort to reach this goal there must be no settling into stagnation. The peace societies especially must work with all their might to get friends of peace into parliament, and subscribe to enable them to take part in the interparliamentary meetings. It would, of course, be still better if the means for their attendance were supplied by a public grant.

Here the NORWEGIAN STORTING has set an example which will be to its honour for all time ; for after about sixty members had joined the interparliamentary union, and chosen Messrs. Ullmann, Horst and Lund as representatives to the conference in London, 1890 ; and after the Arbitration resolution moved had been adopted by the Storting (voted July 2nd, 1890, by eighty votes against twenty-nine), a subsidy of 1,200 kroner was granted for the travelling expenses of the three delegates to the London conference.

This is probably the first time in the life of the nations that a State has granted money in support of a direct effort to make a breach in the old system of Cain.

There is less strain in America : a similar inception seems to be at hand. Long before the great rousing in 1887, the present United States Minister, JAMES G. BLAINE, was possessed with the idea of bringing about a peace-treaty between all the independent States of North and South America. He stood at the head of the Foreign Department of the Union when General Garfield was President, 1881, and already at that time entertained this grand idea. He desired, in order to realize it, to invite all the American States, by means of government emissaries, to take part in an international congress at Washington. In the interim Garfield died, and when Arthur became President, Blaine ceased to be Minister of Foreign Affairs ; but as soon as, upon Harrison being chosen to the presidency, he became Foreign Minister again, he resumed the interrupted work.

In June, 1888, the President confirmed a resolution adopted by Congress, empowering him to invite all the American States to a conference composed of emissaries from their governments, with the view of establishing a Tribunal of Arbitration for settling differences that may arise between them ; and for establishing by commercial treaties more facile trade combinations, adapted to the needs of the various States, and their productive and economic well-being.

The invitations were issued, and met with approval by all the independent States throughout America.

The representatives of these States met at Washington, Oct. 1st, 1889, in a deliberative assembly, which was styled the PAN-AMERICAN CONFERENCE. Mr. Blaine was voted to the chair, and under his leading the members of the congress decided to begin with a circular tour of forty days through the whole of the States of the Union. Its labours were afterwards continued until April 18th, 1890.

The results of the Conference as regards the common interests of trade and commerce, etc., will only be felt gradually, since many of these matters are of intricate character, and in some instances require entirely fresh international transactions. But as regards the chief thing— viz., the establishment of a permanent tribunal of arbitration—the object was achieved.

Congress almost unanimously[1] adopted the resolution of the report of the committee respecting the election of such a supreme judicial authority in case of any menacing international disagreement.

The members of the Conference were not authorized to conclude binding treaties. Their task was confined to deliberating upon affairs

---

[1] The scruples entertained by Chili, Argentina and Mexico appear to have been dropped, in the case at least of the two last named.

which might have a reciprocal interest in various countries, and then laying before their governments such resolutions as in the opinion of the Conference might best promote the well-being of all the States.

Nevertheless the majority of the States later bound themselves to the conclusions of the congress.   Indeed, a week before the assembly broke up the respective members for Brazil, Bolivia, Columbia, Equador, Guatemala, Hayti, Honduras, Nicaragua and Salvador, were empowered to sign at Washington the arbitration-treaty adopted by the Pan-American Conference ; and the other governments have since in the same way sanctioned it.[1]

When this document has been fully confirmed, a quarter of the inhabited world will be rendered inviolate, and 120 millions of men set free from the chronic frenzy of war.

If minor breaches of the peace possibly may not thereby be for ever prevented, yet certainly the irresponsible system of violence will become powerless against the force of civilization which is spreading over the whole Western hemisphere.

[1] For provisions of this Treaty see Appendix.

THE PROSPECTS.

THE events which I have here described will
perhaps one day be regarded as the transition
into a new era. But specially here, in the
Old World, with its many unsettled accounts,
we cannot rely upon bright pictures of the
future. We are convinced of nothing beyond
the range of our own knowledge and experience.

I have thought so myself, and therefore I
have endeavoured to keep to facts which no
one can deny.

It is a fact that WARS CONTINUALLY DIMINISH
in proportion as peoples are brought nearer, to
one another by trade and commerce. The old
warlike condition has ceased. Formerly not a
year passed without war in Europe—in the
Middle Ages hardly a week. After 1815 an
international peace reigned over most of the
European States for forty years. In the Scandinavian peninsula that peace is continuing still.
Before that time, at least until 1721, Sweden

was almost continually involved in war. We reckon two hundred and sixty years of war to the Kalmar Union, and the proneness to invade and defend the countries on the other side the Baltic.

The old CAUSES OF WAR ARE BEING REMOVED. Certainly new ones arise as a result of selfish patriotism, breaking out in new acts of violence. But these outbreaks of barbarism become continually more rare. Unhappily, they are so much the more horrible when they do occur, but yet much more transitory. This is applicable to all the great wars in the last half of the present century. No thirty years' war is known now.

In consequence of the shorter flow of blood the wounds get time to heal, and the divided interests are allowed to grow together again. The levers of civilization are again in motion ; commerce spreads over land and sea by steam, electricity, and other motive powers. The victories of Alexander and Napoleon are cast into the shade by the triumphal procession of the tiny postage stamp around the world. Trade and industry, art and science, efforts in the direction of universal morality and enlight-

enment, all branch out and weave around
the nations a boundless web of common interests, which, though at certain intervals violently
torn asunder by brute force, grows together
again with increased strength and in broader
compass; until one day, under the majesty of
law, it will form an irresistible civilizing
power.

This is what in REALITY IS TAKING PLACE.
Men do not in general see it; and this, because
they busy themselves so much with warlike
notions, and trouble themselves so little about
events of the character that I have dwelt upon
in the foregoing pages.

The friends of peace ought to stimulate one
another, especially when there is gloom over the
great world, and no one knows whence the approaching calamity may spring. Once it was
warded off from our land by a wise measure of
one of our kings. I refer to Oscar I., when he
saved us from being embroiled in the chances
of war, by drawing up a DECLARATION OF NEU-
TRALITY in 1854, which was approved by the
united powers, and earned for him the homage
and gratitude of the Swedish Riksdag, in an

address which lauded him as one of the wisest and noblest of kings.[1]

But there is little security that the same ex-pedient will always lead to a like successful result, if people wait till war is at the door before setting to work.

[1] Transactions of the Riksdag, 1853–1854, No. 4. In the introduction to the address to the Riksdag the king observed, that he had, in providing for the welfare of the nation, found himself obliged to declare Sweden neutral ; consequently he informed the Riksdag of the Declaration of Neutrality, respecting which the king said :—

"The system which the king intends steadily to adhere to and employ is a strict neutrality, founded upon sincerity, impartiality, and full regard to the rights of all the powers. This neutrality will entail upon the government of his Majesty of Sweden and Norway the following duties, and secure to it the following benefits : 1. To hold himself free from any participation in any contentions which directly or indirectly may be advantageous to one and injurious to another of the belligerent States. . . .

"Such are the general principles of the neutral position, which his Majesty of Sweden and Norway designs to take in case war should break out in Europe. His Majesty feels persuaded that it will be accepted as in accordance with international law, and that the exact and impartial observance of these principles will make it possible for his Majesty to continue to sustain those connections with friendly and allied powers which his Majesty, for his people's weal, so greatly desires to preserve from every infringement."

To this communication, satisfactory answers, accepting

In time of peace, and during the specially
good relations which obtain between the two
English-speaking nations, as well as between
France and America, our fellow-workers on
the decision announced by his Majesty, arrived from the
various Governments in the following words: .   .   .

" His Majesty has been pleased to announce to the assembled Estates of the Realm the attainment of this result, so
satisfactory for the undisturbed continuance of peaceful
transactions and the uninterrupted course of trade and
navigation ; so much the more as on account of the political relations of Sweden and Norway with foreign powers,
they may be regarded as for the present amply secured.   His
Majesty gratefully acknowledges that the patriotism and the
reliance upon the paternal designs of his Majesty which
the Estates of the Realm have manifested on this occasion
may be regarded as having in an important degree contributed to the attainment of the desired object.   His Majesty,
in expressing his sincere satisfaction, will continue to devote
incessant pains to all the measures which the maintenance
of neutrality may require in harmony with the principles
laid down and promulgated by his Majesty.   With his
Majesty's royal favour and constant best wishes to the
Estates of the Realm."

The address of thanks from the Riksdag to the king :—

"After the Declaration of Neutrality made by your Majesty
on behalf of the united kingdoms, and in concert with the
King of Denmark, had been accepted by the European
powers and also the United States, it pleased your Majesty
to inform the Estates of the Realm of this result, so satisfactory for the undisturbed continuance of our peaceful
transactions, and for the uninterrupted course of our trade

both sides the Atlantic are making use of the favourable opportunity for trying to get this good relation established by law.

It may well be asked why we, who are

and navigation.   Your Majesty has at the same time been pleased also to express your gracious appreciation of the patriotism and reliance upon your paternal designs which the Estates of the Realm have on this occasion manifested.

"The representatives of the Swedish people hold in grateful remembrance these expressions of your Majesty's high satisfaction, and beg respectfully to assure your Majesty of their deep and warm gratitude.   The Fatherland is indebted to your Majesty's incessant and unremitting pains in securing the friendly relations of the united kingdoms towards foreign powers during the contests in which a great part of Europe is at present embroiled.   The Estates of the Realm offer sincere homage to the resolution and wise forethought with which your Majesty, under these troublous conditions, has safeguarded the interests, the independence and power of the united kingdoms.   With confidence between the king and the people, with mutual co-operation in working together to promote the true welfare of our beloved Fatherland, they will, with the blessing of the Highest, be henceforth preserved.   The peace we enjoy is the dearer because it is the evidence of the fidelity with which the best interests of the country are guarded by your Majesty. Ready to follow her noble king in all vicissitudes, the Swedish nation implores the blessings of Providence upon the vigilant fatherly love whose untiring care for the people's welfare reaps its reward in this answering love.

" The Estates of the Realm, remain," etc.

friendly with the whole world, should not be able to do the same, not only with respect to Siam, but also first and foremost with our near neighbours.

It was this thought which led to the Arbitration resolution in 1890, in the Storting and in the Riksdag.

At the first meeting of the Left (Liberals) of the Storting, Feb. 4th, the subject was discussed and gained unanimous adhesion. Whereupon followed the resolution in the Storting on the 21st, which was adopted by a large majority, March 5th, after the Minister of State (Stang) had delivered a long speech against the resolution in vain.

After this successful result, a similar resolution for Sweden was brought into the First Chamber by F. T. Borg, and in the Second by J. Andersson. The reports of the committees upon it ran diversely. The committee of the First Chamber opposed, and that of the Second Chamber approved, the resolution. On May 12th the question was thrown out in both Chambers.[1]

[1] Riksdagen protocol, 1890. First Chamber, No. 37 ; Second Chamber, No. 45.

Mr. Borg spoke with dignity for his resolution in a long speech. This was answered by the chairman of the committee, with a reminder of the perverse condition of the world and of the human race. The resolution contained a "meaningless expression of opinion." It was a real danger for small nations to go to sleep, hoping and believing in a lasting peace. It was now just as in the olden times : those who loved peace and would preserve it "must prepare for war." The speaker had, as chairman of the committee, expressed sympathy with the resolution, but he added, "one does not get far with paper and words ; and, according to my opinion, the honourable mover of the resolution will certainly show more love for peace if he, next year, on coming back with this peace business, will set about it with a proposition for some ironclads and artillery regiments or such like things, of more effectual service than the platonic love which he has expressed ; and I venture to predict that both the committee and the Chamber will support him more powerfully than to-day."

After another distinguished genius had expressed himself in the same well-known fashion, wherein proofs were conspicuous by their absence, and the narrow circle of thought was filled with scorn and slighting talk about "pious notions," etc., the High Chamber threw out the bill by fifty-six votes against four.

In the Second Chamber the debate was opened by the Foreign Minister with a speech which clearly enough justifies the "MEMORIAL DIPLOMATIQUE" where it points to the necessity of the study of the arbitration-system having a high place amongst the requirements made of those who enter the path of diplomacy ;— a thing that they have actually begun seriously to set before themselves in England.

In full accord with the evidence brought forward above, the judicial professor of the Chamber declared in short that the Chamber would disgrace itself by adopting the resolution before it.

After the mover of the resolution and some who shared his views had expressed their hope that the Chamber would not fall back from the position it took in 1874 upon this question, a speaker rose who requires to be met, Herr A. Hedin.

He began with the assertion that if a refusal

of the report of the committee would show that
the Chamber had now changed its opinion, they
had before them sufficient reason for this. He
wondered that a resolution of such a nature as
this had been brought forward, so soon after
the unpleasant experience which the country
and people of Sweden lately had in a so-called
decision by arbitration. " The Chamber will
please to remember," continued the speaker,
" that the king, with no authority from the
Riksdag, agreed with Spain to appeal to arbitration upon the difficulties that had arisen on
the right understanding of the prolonged commercial treaty with Spain. Also the Chamber
will please to remember that this arbitration
tribunal neither acted upon the plan settled in
the agreement, nor did it act in harmony with
the instructions of the treaty ; and what was
worse, the so-called, or supposed, sentence
which this one-man arbitration tribunal passed
did not concern the matter, which according to
the agreement was to have been settled by
arbitration, but quite another, which could not
reasonably be subjected to arbitration—though
the matter was, so far as we were legally concerned, made to appear as though Sweden had

received an injustice in the principal matter which should have been tried by arbitration, but which was not—a circumstance which, with the Spanish authorities, has greatly weakened the position in law due to Swedish citizens, whose rights have been violated in so unprecedented a manner by the mode of procedure in consequence of which arbitration was appealed to."

All this had truth in it. But does that prove anything against the usefulness of arbitration clauses in treaties of commerce ?

The agreement referred to between the united kingdoms and Spain, January 8th, 1887, establishes :—

"A question which affects customs or the carrying out of commercial treaties, or relates to results of some special violation of the same, shall, when all attempts to come to an amicable agreement and all friendly discussions have proved fruitless, be referred to an arbitration tribunal, whose decision shall be binding on both parties."

According to this it may be plainly seen, that the well-known Swedo-Spanish SPIRIT-DISPUTE, to which Mr. Hedin alluded, ought to have been solved in its entirety by arbitration. The Spanish Government, however, maintained that

this affected Spanish internal concerns, since in
fact the forced sale of Karlstamms-Volagets
brandy stores in Spain took place as a result of
a new spirit law, to which the arbitration clause
in this case could not be applied.

This starting-point for the judgment of the
whole dispute was accepted by the Swedish
Government; which also agreed to let an arbitrator settle whether the question of the spirit
tax was independent of the treaty or not. Both
Governments agreed to choose the Portuguese
ex-Foreign Minister, Count de Casal Riberio,
as arbitrator, and he expressed himself in favour
of the Spanish construction. And with this
the whole matter was settled.

No one can seriously think that the method
of procedure on the Swedish side, which led to
so distressing a violation of justice as that referred to by Herr Hedin, could prove anything
against the principle of arbitration. On the
other hand, it appears to betray the character
of the statesmanship of our then Foreign
Minister; which indeed earned for him a
diamond-set snuffbox from the Emperor
William II., but otherwise, the blame only of
sensible people.

Herr Hedin, who has a weakness for strong expressions, had the opportunity of using some such in their right place.   Unhappily, this cannot be said with truth of the closing words of his speech, where he remarks that the expressions of the Foreign Minister are so decisive against the bill that they deal the report of the committee of the Second Chamber a right deadly blow.

The committee had proposed that the king, with the authority which § 11 in the form of government accords him, should seek to bring about such agreements with foreign powers, that future possible differences between the powers named and Sweden should be settled by arbitration.

The deadly blow must be the remark of the Foreign Minister that questions affecting the *existence and independence of nations* must be excepted from decisions by arbitration.

This principle is known to be universally accepted, and in no way stands in antagonism to the report of the committee, which of course left the hands of the king as free as possible to promote the idea of arbitration according to circumstances.

However, the report of the committee was thrown out by eighty-eight votes against eighty-three.

Herr Hedin got his way. He has always been the consistent opposer of the active friends of peace ; and this time he has besides won the gratitude even of our Government organ, *Nya Dagligt Allehanda*, which calls his speech glittering ; meaning that upon this resolution " there was no need to waste many words," and continues thus :—

"The resolution is worthy of notice, because it shows the return of the Chamber to a sounder perception of this question. It seems at last to recognise the extravagance of the expectation certain fanatics entertain of bringing about a lasting peace by so apparently simple a means as a tribunal of arbitration. We have indeed, as Herr Hedin reminded us, now had experience ourselves of how unsatisfactory this can be ; and it certainly appears that they must be lacking in common sense who would question the justice of the Foreign Minister's reminder, that arbitration cannot be appealed to when a nation's political freedom or independence is touched by the issue."

I may here beg leave to calm the ruffled feelings of the honourable Government organ by bringing to remembrance the lesson, otherwise applicable also, which our dismembered sister-land on the other side of the Sound offers us.

At the London Conference in 1864, the representative of England, Lord Russell, referred to the decision arrived at by the Paris Congress in 1856, that States which had any serious dispute should appeal to the mediation of a friendly power before taking to arms. In harmony with this the British plenipotentiary proposed that the question, whether the boundary line should be drawn between the lines of Aabenraa-Tœnder, on the one side, or Danne-werke-Sli on the other, should be decided by arbitration. Prussia and Austria consented to accept the mediation of a neutral power; but Denmark replied to the proposition with a distinct refusal. In the same way Denmark refused the proposal made first by Prussia, and later by France, that a means of deciding the boundary should be sought in a plebiscite of the people in Sleswick.

Denmark trusted too much upon might and too little upon right. Otherwise Sleswick had still been Danish.

If the axiom be correct, that disputes which affect the existence and independence of nations ought not to be submitted for solution to arbitration, it is of so much the greater moment to try to get international complications settled in this way, because they may swell up into questions of the kind first named ; since in any case this means could be adopted as a last re-source in time of need. History knows of no example of the destruction of a free nation by the impartial judgment of arbitration.

Now it may well appear honourable on the part of the free nations of the Scandinavian peninsula that they should openly show to the whole world that they are prepared (in full harmony with King Oscar II.'s pacific expres-sions in the speech from the throne to the Riksdag and the Storting in 1890), for their own part, in all international circumstances to substitute justice for brute force,—and this with-out compromising and meaningless limitations. In the Swedish arbitration resolution, as well as in the Norse, lies the road certainly to effi-ciently carrying out the neutral policy so strongly emphasized in the speech from the throne. Besides the public gain, which a favourable result in both Chambers would have been, a unanimous co-operation in this cause would in a great degree have facilitated the solving of the important QUESTION of the UNION (UNION-ELLE TVISTEMAAL).

The last named consideration will indeed claim more attention as the consequences of the divergent decisions of the Storting and the Riksdag develop themselves. That these consequences will be scattering, rather than uniting, the friends of peace in both lands must keep in view ; and must look out, in time, for means to soothe them, as long as they continue.

That which lies nearest my heart has been to help, with cheering words, to strengthen the faith of my fellow-workers. If these words have succeeded also, here and there, in scattering doubts, so much the better. Little-faith is faint-hearted. Without confidence in a cause, there is no action. Ignorance may be enlightened, superstition wiped out ; intolerance may become tolerant, and hate be changed into love ; ideas may be quickened, intelligence widened, and men's hearts may be ennobled ; but from *pessimism* which can see nothing but gloomy visions nothing is to be expected. This offspring of materialism is one of the most powerful opponents which the cause of international law and justice has to encounter. It is only self-deception to conceal the fact that it still reigns in our Christian community.

These gloomy-sighted people refer us to history, which on every page tells of crime and blood, sorrow and tears. We answer by pointing to the development of civilization, and show how all things slowly grow and ripen, whether in human life or in the world of nature.

Human perfection does not provide for an individual being a law-abiding member of a human community, and exclude a community from being a law-abiding member of an alliance of States. The abolition of war therefore in no way pre-supposes universal righteousness, but only a certain degree of moral cultivation.

But that this perfection is not attained to cannot be any rational objection *against* striving after the perfect. Discontent with imperfection ought much rather to goad us on to work for what is better.

Now, war is not something imperfect only: it is a summing up of all human depravity—

a condition which we might expect all enlightened men and women would turn against
with combined energies. That this does not
take place is an evidence that the enlighten-
ment is not so great among so-called cultivated
people.

The dazzling external show of war conceals
from many its inner reality. This applies not
only to the horrors of the battle-field and their
ghastly accompaniments. Fancy's wildest pictures of the infernal abyss are nothing to the
descriptions eye-witnesses give of this veritable
hell. Tolstoï's pen and Veretschagin's pencil
give us an idea of it.[1] From this misery spring
untold sufferings for thousands upon thousands
of innocent victims ; and, besides, it remains to
be a flowing source of fresh calamities.

The ARMED PEACE is a similar calamity,
which threatens European civilization with
complete overthrow. We have got so far in
the general race in the science of armaments
that the yearly outlay in Europe for military
purposes, including the interest of national

[1] When Wellington once, as a victor, went over the field
of battle, he burst out with the cry, "There is nothing so
disastrous as a victory, except a defeat."

debts, is reckoned as about twelve milliards of kroner,[1] 650 millions sterling, which of course must imply a corresponding limitation of productive labour.

In time of peace the European armies are reckoned at four millions of men. In time of war this can grow to nineteen millions; and in a few years when, as intended, the new conscription law comes into full effect, to something like thirty millions.[2]

War, the personification of all human depravity, desolates the progressive work of culture, and the armed peace which ruins the nations prepares new wars and augments the misery. Ignorance, war, and poverty follow one another in an unvarying circle.

By the side of this wild race for armaments goes on a terrible struggle for existence, and discontent reigns in all lands. This condition of things, which fills the world with unrest and fear, must in the near future have an end. It

[1] That is 12,000,000,000; sufficient to furnish the annual pension of a minister of State, 2,000 kroner, for EVERY man and woman, old man and suckling in the whole of Norway. — ED. of Danish edition.

[2] Five times as many able-bodied men as there are men, women, old men and children in the whole of Norway.—Do.

will either come in the form of a social revolution, which will embrace the whole of our continent, or it may come by the introduction of
an established condition of international law.

It is the last named outcome that active
friends of peace labour for. They strive to
enlighten the nations as to the means of re-
moving and preventing these calamities ; and
they hope that the so-called educated classes
will cease to be inactive spectators of these
efforts. While they do not feel called upon to
oppose the nonsense of folly, they listen respectfully to objections dictated by a sincere patriotism. In that feeling we ought all to be able
to join. It depends upon the way in which
this is expressed whether we can work together or must go on separate lines.

Commonly, we commend an action as vir-
tuous when it does not oppose our interests,
but brand it as blameworthy when it in some
way threatens our position.

Thus we read, with glad appreciation, the
deeds of our own warriors; but our admiration
is changed into resentment when the exploits
are achieved against ourselves by the heroes of
other nations. When one says in Sweden, " I

am not a Russian, indeed"; they say in Russia,
"You behave yourself like a Swede." It
needs an independent third party to give an
impartial judgment.   Right must be right.

If our so-called enemy is *really* in the right,
he does not become wrong *because* he is called
our enemy; and if we conquer and kill him, we
only thereby increase a hundredfold our terrible
guilt.   It is in the long run a loss to both sides.
Here, at any rate at least, a *compromise* is
needed, for it is seldom the fault of *one* when
two quarrel.

But the endeavour to get a permanent arbitration tribunal established cannot, in any way,
be reasonably opposed to efforts for the welfare
of one's own country.   The very conscious-
ness of the existence of such a tribunal would
little by little, as a matter of course, bring about
the reign of law.   It would indeed be a marvellous perversion of ideas which esteemed it
dishonourable to feel bound, in case of disputes
with other countries, to appeal to law and
justice; inasmuch as this very unwillingness to
seek the path of justice must excite a serious
suspicion as to the cause you maintain.

To lay hold on the sword under the influence

of passion is like taking a knife when intoxi-
cated; and it is a crying absurdity to expect
people, who soberly know what they are doing,
to go to homicide with a light heart. That is
to say, that a good man in severe conflict as to
his duty, may possibly be forced to do a bad
action to escape participation in a still worse.
If he forbears to kill his brother, this last will
murder his father. When warriors are led out
to battle, the brilliant uniform ought to be laid
aside, and the troops clad in sombre mourning,
which would better accord with the naked
reality. When they have slain many and come
back in triumph, decorated with honourable
Cain-badges, they are wont in their homes to
point with pride to their brothers who lie silent
in their blood. They earn a character for
having done something great; they are received
with exultation and honourable distinctions, and
praised as gods in popular story. But the
whole spirit and conception is false IF Christ's
teaching of love is true; and we should long
since have grown out of this heathenish religion
if there had not been incorporated with it so
much patriotism, both true and false—the false
wrapped in those high sounding words and

phrases of self-love and vanity which still exercise so great a power over the easily excited spirit of the nations.

But if we set our thoughts free, confined as they are by warm devotion to our hereditary soil, and now and then venture to look out over the wide world, we shall see points of contact in the progressive effort of humanity; and it is our highest honour to be able to take an active part in this. Barriers are crumbling away one after the other. They do not go down with violence; they vanish as new ideas smooth the way for a higher conception of human dignity. Inquiry dissipates prejudice, and continually shows us new phases of the inner cohesion of the life of nations.

The inhabitants of Europe, says DRAPER, show a constantly increasing disposition towards the complete levelling of their mutual dissimilarities. Climatic and meteorological differences are more and more dissolved by artificial means and new inventions; and thence arises a similarity, not only in habits of life, but in physical conformation. Such inventions soften the influences to which men are subjected, and bring them nearer to an average type. With this

M

greater affinity one to the other in bodily form, follows also a greater similarity in feeling, habit and thought.

Day by day, too, the economic fellowship of Europe increases. Communications by ship, railroad, post and telegraph are developed; by means of State loans, share and exchange connections, interests are knit together. Therefore we see the Bourse, the barometer of economic life, fluctuate when serious rumours of war are afloat; an evidence that common economic interests and war are at variance one with the other.

I shall not venture further, but simply indicate in closing that even the differences in language will certainly go on being gradually adjusted.

It is a remarkable fact, says the above-named investigator, that in nearly all Indo-Germanic races, family appellatives, father, mother, sister, brother, daughter, are the same. A similar agreement may be observed in the names of a great number of everyday things, such as house, door, way; but one finds that whilst these observations hold good in respect to the designation of objects of a peaceful character, many of the words which have a military signification are different in the different languages.

Here lies, perhaps, the germ of a future progressive growth which will rise higher heavenward than the tower of Babel.

I believe, for my part, that the English language, both on the ground of its cosmopolitan character and of its great expansion, is already on the path of transition into a universal common language. According to Mulhall, it has spread since 1801, 310 per cent., whilst German has increased 70, and French 36 per cent. A hundred years ago, Gladstone says, the English tongue was spoken by fifteen millions; it is now spoken by 150 millions; and according to the computation of Barham Zincke, in another hundred it will be spoken by at least 1,000 millions.

The computation is probably correct; and then not only in America, but in every part of our globe, the remembrance will be treasured of the little flock of Puritans who, ere they landed from their frail *Mayflower* upon the desolate rocks of a strange coast, drew up in that undeveloped language the great social law for their future, which begins with the words, "In the name of God be it enacted."

Mankind will hold them in remembrance for their faith in a high ideal, these persecuted, weary, sick, and hungry men. For it was that faith which upheld them under continued trials and sufferings, and brought them a victory guiltless of blood, but fraught with blessing to coming generations.

Even if many of us do not believe in the way those Christian heroes believed, yet we may in this materialistic age have strong confidence in the power of good, and so pronounced, that we shall gain something for our cause.

In the life of Society, however, as in external nature with all its teeming variety, we observe a subserviency to law, which may be taken as the surest pledge of the final triumph of the cause of peace.

For my part, I see herein the Divine government of the world.

And therefore my love for this idea can never be extinguished.

APPENDIX.

Note on page 123.

The ASSOCIATION for the NEUTRALIZATION of DENMARK.
The objects of this Association are to work for :

1. Securing for Denmark a permanent neutrality recognised by Europe, like that of Belgium or Switzerland ;

2. The concluding of Arbitration treaties between Denmark and other independent States, especially the two Northern Kingdoms ;

3. The solution by a pacific means of the North Sleswick question in accordance with the principle of popular veto.

Note on page 125.

INTERNATIONAL ARBITRATION and PEACE ASSOCIATION (40 and 41, Outer Temple, London, W.C.).

OBJECTS.

Among the objects of this Association are the following :

1. To create, educate, and organize public opinion throughout Europe in favour of the substitution of ARBITRATION for WAR.

2. To promote a better understanding and more friendly feeling between the citizens of different nations.

3. To correct erroneous statements in the public press or in Parliaments on International questions.

MODES OF ACTION.

1. To establish in the chief cities of Europe Committees or Societies which shall correspond with each other on all matters likely to create disputes, with the view of ascertaining the facts and of suggesting just and practical modes of settlement.

2. Where Committees cannot at present be formed, to obtain the services of individuals acting in co-operation for the same purpose.

3. To form a medium of communication between men of different countries by a Journal devoted to these purposes, and to promote International fraternity and co-operation, mutual appreciation and esteem.

4. To hold periodical conferences and congresses in all parts of Europe.

5. To correspond and work with similar Associations and committees in America.

WHAT THE ASSOCIATION HAS DONE.

It has held two International Congresses on the European continent. Many visits have been paid to cities in Germany, Italy, France, Switzerland, Belgium, Austria, and Hungary, for the above purpose. In these countries, including America, the Association has directly or indirectly corresponded with more than six hundred persons, many of whom are Members of Parliament, journalists, literary men, professors, merchants, and manufacturers.

Corresponding Committees and Societies have been founded by the Association in Germany, Hungary, Italy and France; and Societies are affiliated in Belgium, Norway, Sweden, Denmark, and California.

WHAT IT DESIRES TO DO.

To complete the "International Federation" of Peace-makers pro posed by the Congress held at Berne in 1883.

To promote the formation of Societies belonging to this Federation in all parts of Europe.

To form Branches of the Association in various parts of England.

To publish a foreign edition of the monthly paper, *Concord*, in French and German.

Note on page 137.

The following are the provisions of the Treaty agreed to at the PAN-AMERICAN CONFERENCE.

Article I.—The republics of North, Central, and South America hereby adopt arbitration as a principle of American International Law for the settlement of all differences, disputes, or controversies that may arise between them.

Article II.—Arbitration shall be obligatory in all controversies concerning diplomatic and consular privileges, boundaries, territories, indemnities, the right of navigation, and the validity, construction, and enforcement of treaties.

Article III.—Arbitration shall be equally obligatory in all cases other than those mentioned in the foregoing article, whatever may be their origin, nature, or occasion; with the single exception mentioned in the next following article.

Article IV.—The sole questions excepted from the provisions of the preceding article are those which, in the judgment of any one of the nations involved in the controversy, may imperil its independence. In which case, for such nation, arbitration shall be optional; but it shall be obligatory upon the adversary power.

Article V.—All controversies or differences, with the exception stated in Article IV., whether pending or hereafter arising, shall be submitted to arbitration, even though they may have originated in occurrences ante-dating the present treaty.

Article VI.—No question shall be revived by virtue of this treaty concerning which a definite agreement shall already have been reached. In such cases arbitration shall be resorted to only for the settlement of questions concerning the validity, interpretation, or enforcement of such agreements.

Article VII.—Any Government may serve in the capacity of arbitrator which maintains friendly relations with the nation opposed to the one selecting it. The office of arbitrator may also be entrusted to tribunals of justice, to scientific bodies, to public officials, or to private individuals, whether citizens or not of the States selecting them.

Article VIII.—The court of arbitration may consist of one or more persons. If of one person, he shall be selected jointly by the nations concerned. If of several persons, their selection may be jointly made by the nations concerned. Should no choice be made, each nation claiming a distinct interest in the question at issue shall have the right to appoint one arbitrator on its own behalf.

Article IX.—When the court shall consist of an even number of arbitrators, the nations concerned shall appoint an umpire, who shall decide all questions upon which the arbitrators may disagree. If the nations interested fail to agree in the selection of an umpire, such umpire shall be selected by the arbitrators already appointed.

Article X.—The appointment of an umpire, and his acceptance, shall take place before the arbitrators enter upon the hearing of the question in dispute.

Article XI.—The umpire shall not act as a member of the court, but his duties and powers shall be limited to the decision of questions upon which the arbitrators shall be unable to agree.

Article XII.—Should any arbitrator, or an umpire, be prevented from serving by reason of death, resignation, or other cause, such arbitrator or umpire shall be replaced by a substitute to be selected in the same manner in which the original arbitrator or umpire shall have been chosen.

Article XIII.—The court shall hold its sessions at such place as the parties in interest may agree upon, and in case of disagreement or failure to name a place the court itself may determine the location.

Article XIV.—When the court shall consist of several arbitrators, a majority of the whole number may act notwithstanding the absence or withdrawal of the minority. In such case the majority shall continue in the performance of their duties, until they shall have reached a final determination of the questions submitted for their consideration.

Article XV.—The decision of a majority of the whole number of arbitrators shall be final both on the main and incidental issues, unless in the agreement to arbitrate it shall have been expressly provided that unanimity is essential.

Article XVI.—The general expenses of arbitration proceedings shall be paid in equal proportions by the governments that are parties thereto ; but expenses incurred by either party in the preparation and prosecution of its case shall be defrayed by it individually.

Article XVII.—Whenever disputes arise the nations involved shall appoint courts of arbitration in accordance with the provisions of the preceding articles. Only by the mutual and free consent of all of such nations may those provisions be disregarded, and courts of arbitration appointed under different arrangements.

Article XVIII.—This treaty shall remain in force for twenty years from the date of the exchange of ratifications. After the expiration of that period, it shall continue in operation until one of the contracting parties shall have notified all the others of its desire to terminate it. In the event of such notice the treaty shall continue obligatory upon the party giving it for at least one year thereafter, but the withdrawal of one or more nations shall not invalidate the treaty with respect to the other nations concerned.

Article XIX.—This treaty shall be ratified by all the nations approving it, according to their respective constitutional methods ; and the ratifications shall be exchanged in the city of Washington on or before the first day of May, A.D. 1891. Any other nation may accept this treaty and become a party thereto, by signing a copy thereof and depositing the same with the Government of the United States ; whereupon the said Government shall communicate this fact to the other contracting parties.

Butler & Tanner, The Selwood Printing Works, Frome, and London.